ABC GUIDE TO ANATOMY AND PHYSIO

ABC GUIDE

ANATOMY AND PHYSIOLOGY
FOR HEALTH AND SOCIAL
CARE

Level 3

Mark Walsh

ABC GUIDE TO ANATOMY AND PHYSIOLOGY

Published by Textbook Training *Publishers*
Learning support for health and social care

© Text copyright Mark Walsh 2016

Mark Walsh asserts the moral right to be identified as the author of this work.

All rights reserved.

Also available in this series:

Human Lifespan Development – An ABC Guide for Tutors
ISBN 978-1533355942

Working in Health and Social Care – An ABC Guide for Tutors
ISBN 978-1533356024

Meeting Individual Care and Support Needs – An ABC Guide for Tutors ISBN 978-1533356185

Psychological Perspectives – An ABC Guide for Tutors
ISBN 978-1533082329

Sociological Perspectives – An ABC Guide for Tutors
ISBN 978-1533356208

Email **gnvq@btinternet.com** for a FREE pack of case studies (PDF format)

HEALTH AND SOCIAL CARE

Introduction

This *ABC Guide to Anatomy and Physiology for Health and Social Care* covers 87 entries that define, discuss and explain a range of concepts, terms and theories that feature in the anatomy and physiology units of level 3 health and social care courses. These include *Unit 4 Anatomy and Physiology for Health and Social Care* of the *BTEC National Health and Social Care* course, *Unit 4 Development through the Life Stages* of the *OCR Level 3 Cambridge Technical Health and Social Care* awards. The *ABC Guide to Anatomy and Physiology* has been written to provide learners with a broad ranging resource to support learning within these particular units.

Unlike a textbook, this book is not designed to be read sequentially. You can find and access information about any one entry as the need arises but also follow some links between entries to build up and develop your understanding of a topic area. Try using a particular term as a 'way in' or jumping off point and go from there!

At the end of each entry the *See also* suggestions are used to indicate how the term is connected to other issues, debates and topics within and beyond the unit you are studying. You are encouraged to follow up some of these links and to move between the entries to clarify and deepen your understanding. References are also provided where appropriate and could be followed up as a way of extending your knowledge and understanding if you have a strong interest in a particular topic or issue.

I hope that you find the material in the *ABC Guide* helpful in your studying.

Mark Walsh

Alimentary canal

The alimentary canal is the main physical structure within the digestive system. It is also known as the digestive tract. The alimentary canal includes the mouth, pharynx, oesophagus, stomach, small intestine, large intestine, and the anus.

The alimentary canal is about nine metres long. It extends from your mouth to your anus and is mainly folded and packed neatly inside your abdominal cavity. In a healthy adult, a meal takes between 24 and 72 hours to be fully digested and processed within the alimentary canal. In this time, it will be broken down and absorbed in various ways as it travels through the alimentary canal.

Food begins its digestive journey in the form of large complex molecules of protein, carbohydrate and lipids (fats). In this form nutrients are unable to pass through the lining of the alimentary canal and cannot deliver the energy the body requires. The process of digestion converts these large molecules into simpler, soluble molecules that can be absorbed into the blood stream and distributed to the body's cells for metabolic processes to take place.

HEALTH AND SOCIAL CARE

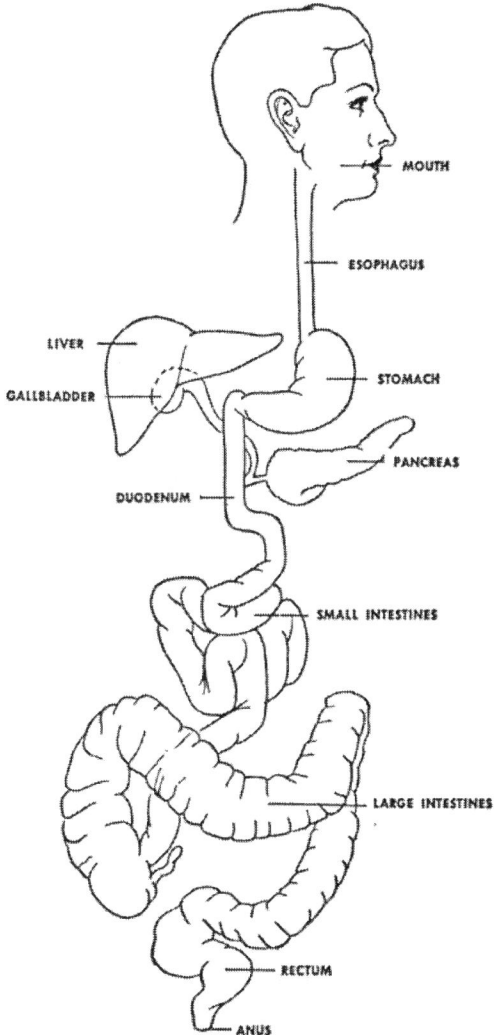

Figure 1 – The alimentary canal consists of a number of different structures.

See also – Digestion; Digestive system; Ileum; Intestines; Stomach

ABC GUIDE TO ANATOMY AND PHYSIOLOGY

Amniocentesis

Amniocentesis is a prenatal (prebirth) medical test that can be used to screen for chromosomal abnormalities associated with Down's syndrome and some other serious health conditions such as Spina bifida, muscular dystrophy and sickle cell anaemia.

An amniocentesis test isn't offered to every pregnant woman in the UK. It is offered to women who are at higher risk of having a baby with a genetic condition. This may be because the woman has previously had a baby with a genetic condition, has terminated an earlier pregnancy because of this or because there is a family history of genetically inherited disorder (cystic fibrosis, Down's syndrome or spina bifida, for example).

Women who are offered the test are able to choose whether to have it or not. Whilst it is relatively safe, there is a low risk that an amniocentesis test can result in a miscarriage so some women choose not to have the test done. Other women choose not to have an amniocentesis because they do not wish to know whether their baby has a chromosomal abnormality or serious health condition or may consider it unethical to abort a foetus for this reason. Where a woman does choose to have the test, it is usually carried out between 15 – 20 weeks into her pregnancy.

The test involves a long, thin needle being inserted through the woman's abdomen into the amniotic sac that surrounds the developing foetus. A small amount of amniotic fluid containing some foetal tissue is drawn out. The foetal DNA is then examined for genetic abnormalities. In most cases, the results of the test are negative – meaning the baby doesn't have any of the disorders being tested for. Where a test is positive, the baby will have one of the disorders being tested for.

HEALTH AND SOCIAL CARE

Healthcare staff will need to explain the implications of this and support the woman in choosing to either continue with or end her pregnancy.

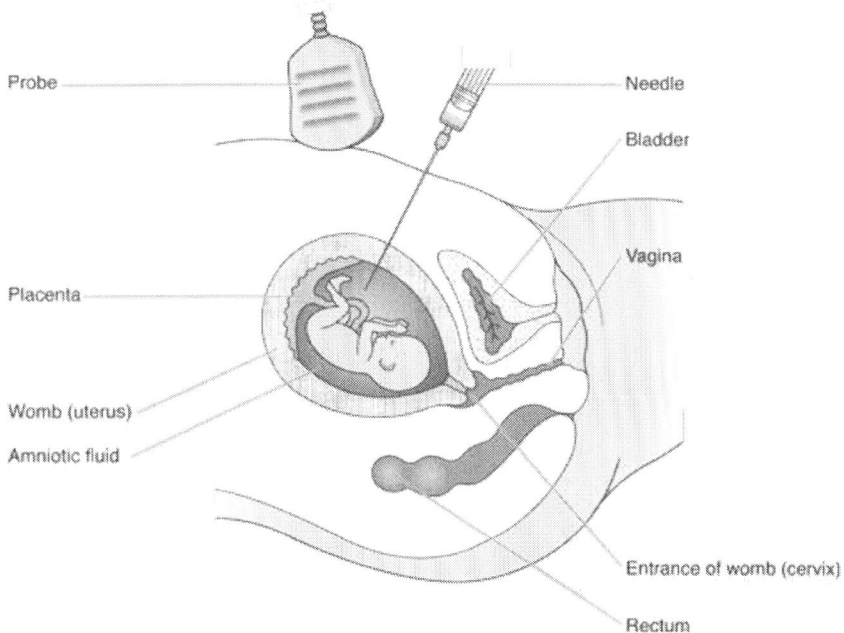

Figure 2 – An illustration of the amniocentesis procedure.

See also – Chorionic villi sampling; Foetal development; Down's syndrome; Cystic fibrosis

ABC GUIDE TO ANATOMY AND PHYSIOLOGY

Anaemia

Anaemia is a general term that refers to a group of disorders that affect the blood cells.

Broadly, the problem is that a person's blood can't carry enough oxygen to meet the needs of their body. This may be because a person has insufficient red blood cells (erythrocytes) or insufficient haemoglobin in their red blood cells. A person may be diagnosed with:

- iron-deficiency anaemia
- megaloblastic anaemia (vitamin B12 anaemia)
- hypoplastic anaemia (inadequately functioning bone marrow)

A person with anaemia may feel tired, short of breath, have palpitations (heart racing / thumping) and look pale. Anaemia is diagnosed through blood tests. Blood is taken and sent to a laboratory for a full blood count (checking haemoglobin levels and the number of blood cells present), a blood film test (checking the size and shape of red blood cells) and the checking of vitamin B12, iron and folate levels.

Treatment depends on the cause of the person's anaemia. In most cases this involves a change in diet or taking supplements because a person needs to increase their iron, vitamin B12 or folic acid levels. In other more serious situations, a blood transfusion may be required but this is rare.

See also – Blood; Cells; Sickle cell disease

HEALTH AND SOCIAL CARE

Anabolism

Anabolism is a set of chemical reactions that happen in the body's cells that support the growth of new cells, the maintenance of body tissues and storage of energy for the future.

Anabolism converts small molecules into larger more complex molecules of carbohydrate, protein and fat. It is a building and storing process and is sometimes also called 'constructive metabolism'.

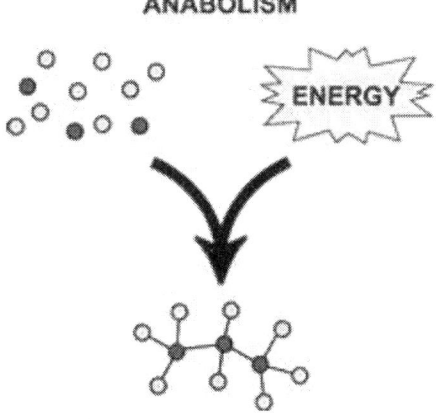

Figure 3 – Anabolism is a constructive building process that occurs at a cellular level

See also – Catabolism; Energy metabolism

ABC GUIDE TO ANATOMY AND PHYSIOLOGY

Asthma

Asthma is a disorder of the respiratory system. It is caused when muscles in the airway constrict (get narrower) because the bronchi have gone into spasm. This then affects airflow and the person's ability to breathe freely and easily.

Asthma attacks typically occur because a person is reacting to pollutants in the air, such as cigarette smoke, vehicle exhaust emissions or dust. Figure 00 described the stages and biological processes that occur when an asthma attack is triggered.

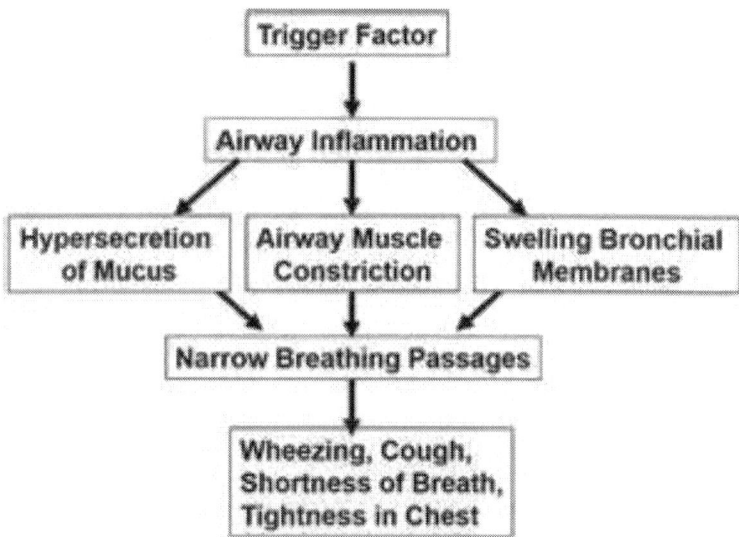

Figure 4 – A number of biological responses occur during an asthma attack

HEALTH AND SOCIAL CARE

Asthma is a relatively common, long-term condition in the United Kingdom. It affects people to varying degrees. Some people have well controlled asthma whilst others experience more persistent difficulties and frequent attacks. Most people are able to manage their own symptoms and prevent asthma attacks by avoiding trigger factors (cigarette smoke, animal fur, intense exercise) and by using inhalers to deliver medication that reduce inflammation and dilate their airways. There are circumstances where a severe asthma attack requires emergency hospital treatment.

See also – Respiratory system; Lungs

ABC GUIDE TO ANATOMY AND PHYSIOLOGY

Autonomic nervous system

The autonomic nervous system is the part of the human peripheral nervous system that communicates nerve impulses ('messages') from the central nervous system to cardiac and smooth muscles.

The function of the autonomic system is to control changes within the body. We do not have any conscious control over these changes and sometimes they can do damage. For example, stress or fear can lead to an increase in heart rate which could, in turn, lead to a heart attack. Strangely, it *is* possible for people to be frightened to death.

The autonomic system is divided into two parts:

- The sympathetic system prepares the body for action – these are the nerves that act when we are under stress. In particular, it is this part of the autonomic nervous system that helps to prepare the body for 'fight or flight'.

- The parasympathetic system is antagonistic to the sympathetic system. 'Antagonistic' means it has the opposite effect so the parasympathetic system helps to calm us down and prepare us for rest. It is the part of the autonomic nervous system that keeps normal body functions running when the body is at rest or in non-threatening, low stress situations.

Figure 5 describes how the two parts of the autonomic nervous system work in opposite ways to each other

HEALTH AND SOCIAL CARE

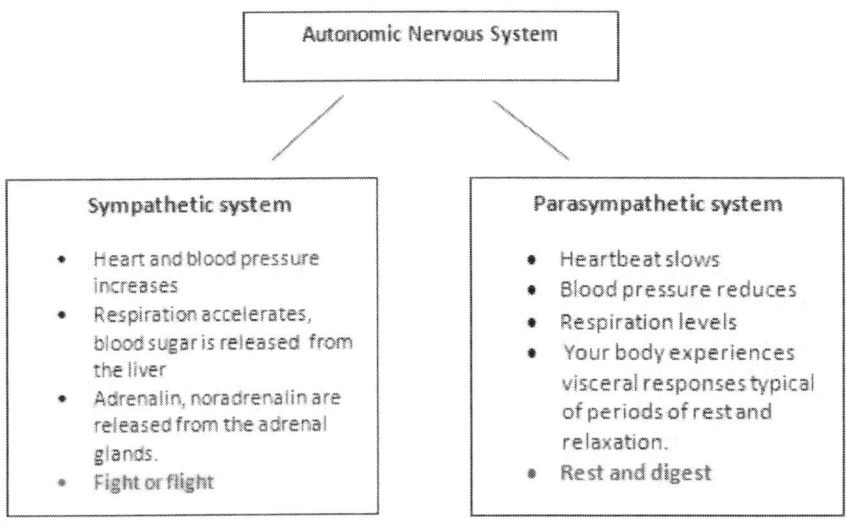

Figure 5 – Each part of the ANS generates the opposite effect to the other.

Filmmakers have known how to control our autonomic nervous system for years. For example, the music, the lighting and the atmosphere of a scary film acts on our autonomic nervous system to make our hearts race, our palms sweat and the hairs on the back of our necks stand up!

See also – Central nervous system; Negative feedback system;

ABC GUIDE TO ANATOMY AND PHYSIOLOGY

Basal metabolic rate (BMR)

The rate at which the human body uses energy is called the metabolic rate. A person's *basal* metabolic rate is the amount of heat (energy) produced by their body after fasting for 12 hours and at rest.

A person's basal metabolic rate will change over their lifespan and varies between individuals. A number of factors affect basal metabolic rate, including:

- Surface area of the body – people with smaller bodies have higher BMR
- Age – children and adolescents have higher BMR
- Thyroxin production – the more of this hormone a person produces, the higher their BMR.

See also- Anabolism; Catabolism; Energy

Bladder

The bladder is the part of the urinary system that collects and temporarily stores urine before it is excreted (removed) from the body. The bladder stretches when it fills and contracts when it is emptied.

The bladder consists of a number of different layers of tissue. The inner lining of the bladder, known as the *transitional epithelium*, stretches as the bladders fills with urine. Its function is to prevent urine being absorbed back into the body. Underneath this layer is the *lamina propria*, a thin layer of connective tissue. Lying underneath this is the *muscularis propria*, a further layer of muscle tissue. A layer of fatty connective tissue surrounds this, separating the bladder from other body organs, particularly the prostate gland and kidneys.

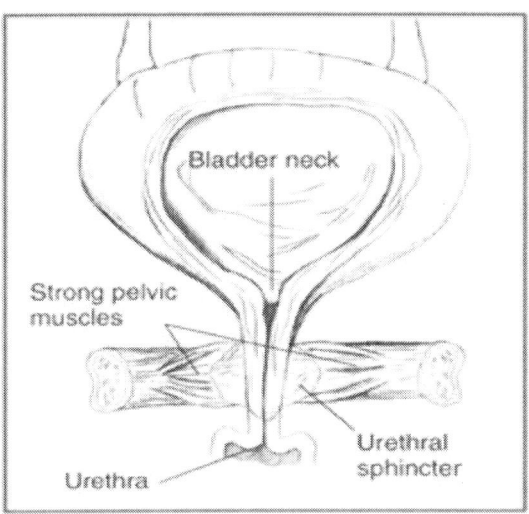

Figure 6 – An illustration of the female bladder

See also – Renal system; Urinary system

ABC GUIDE TO ANATOMY AND PHYSIOLOGY

Blood

Blood is a key body fluid that delivers oxygen and nutrients to the cells and transports waste products away from those cells so that they can be excreted from the body.

A normal adult male will have roughly 6 litres of blood and it will comprise about eight percent of their total body weight. Human blood is a complex mixture of substances that do different jobs. For example, the red cells (erythrocytes) carry oxygen around the body while the white cells (leukocytes) protect against disease.

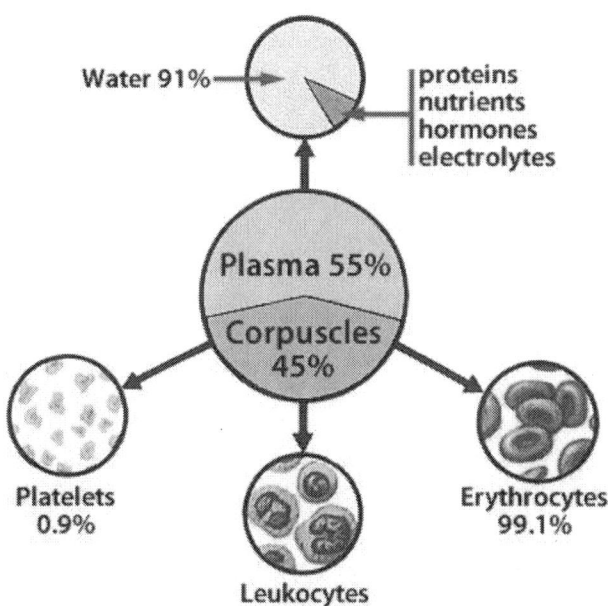

Figure 7 – Human blood consists of a number of different fluids and types of cells

A person's blood is constantly monitored by their body to make sure every single component remains within safe limits. It is a dynamic system with old parts being destroyed and cleared away at the same rate as new parts are made to replace them. No cell in the body is more than 1mm away from the blood. This means that any poisons that get into the blood spread rapidly and dangerously through the body.

Blood glucose levels.

Glucose is the sugar molecule found in human blood. Every cell in the body needs a constant supply of glucose for respiration. The normal range of blood glucose level extends from 70-110mg/100ml of blood and is controlled by two hormones – insulin and glucagon.

Regulation of blood glucose levels

The level of glucose in the blood is controlled by a negative feedback system. The pancreas is the control centre. It monitors how much glucose is in the bloodstream and whether there is sufficient insulin and glucagon to maintain a correct blood sugar level. These hormones act antagonistically to each other – this means they reverse the effects of each other. Insulin is produced by the islets of Langerhans in the pancreas and tends to reduce the level of glucose in the blood while glucagon tends to raise the level of glucose in the blood.

A person's blood glucose level, and their negative feedback system, is affected by food. Shortly after eating a meal a person will have a high blood sugar level. When they are hungry they will have a low blood sugar level

ABC GUIDE TO ANATOMY AND PHYSIOLOGY

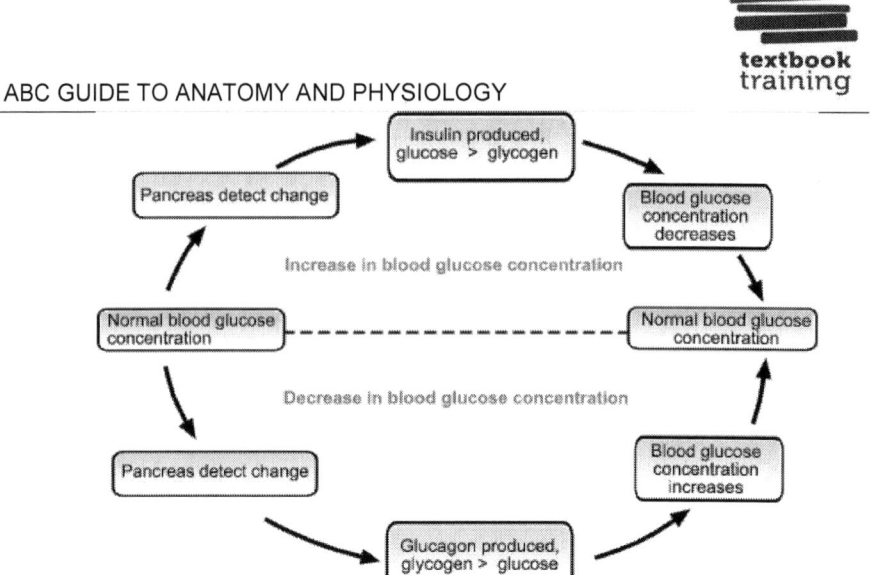

Figure 8 – Blood glucose levels are controlled through a negative feedback system

See also - Anaemia; Blood pressure; Blood vessels; Diabetes; Hodgkin's disease; Leukaemia; Sickle cell disease; Tissues

Blood vessels

A blood vessel is a tube that carries blood through the tissues and organs of the body. There are a number of different types of blood vessels within the human body including arteries, veins and capillaries.

Arteries are the tubes that carry blood away from the heart to organs and tissues around the body. Arteries deliver blood to smaller blood vessels called arterioles that in turn supply capillaries. The pulmonary and umbilical arteries are the exceptions to the rule that arteries carry oxygenated blood. These two arteries carry deoxygenated blood to the lungs (pulmonary) and to the placenta (umbilical) during pregnancy to pick up oxygen.

Veins and smaller venules are the tubes that carry blood from the body back towards the heart. Both arteries and veins can get wider or narrower to control the flow of blood to different organs. When they get wider (or dilate) more blood flows but when they get narrower (or constrict) the blood supply drops. Every major body organ has its own artery and vein.

All the arteries branch off the aorta. When the left ventricle of the heart contracts it pushes a surge of blood into the aorta. The aorta stretches slightly to reduce the effect of the surge. When the ventricle is filling with blood, the walls of the aorta spring back and squeeze on the blood. This stretching and contracting helps to smooth out the flow of the blood but cannot stop it completely. When an artery runs over a bone or near to the surface of the body you can feel the surges through the skin. This is the pulse. Every pulse beat corresponds to a heartbeat.

ABC GUIDE TO ANATOMY AND PHYSIOLOGY

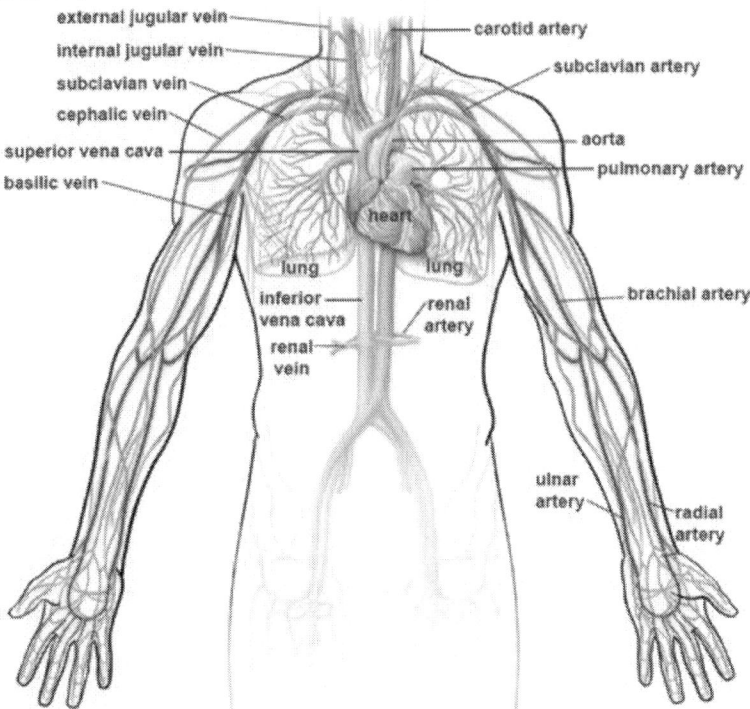

Figure 9 – Blood vessels and arteries of the upper body

Capillaries are the smallest blood vessels in the body and have walls that are only one cell thick. Capillaries join arteries to veins. They carry blood into every part of the body and allow food and oxygen to pass from the blood to the body tissues. Waste products pass the other way. No cell in the body is more than a millimetre away from a capillary.

See also – Blood; Blood pressure; Cardiovascular system; Heart; Stroke.

HEALTH AND SOCIAL CARE

Blood pressure

Blood pressure is the pressure exerted on the walls of the blood vessels by blood circulating within the body.

When a person's blood pressure is checked, two measurements are taken. The force, or pressure, which the blood puts on the walls of the artery when the heart is known as the systolic blood pressure. The continuous pressure that the person's blood puts on the arteries between heart beats is known as the diastolic blood pressure. A person's blood pressure reading is recorded and written as two numbers. The systolic measure comes first, followed by the diastolic measure. On average, a healthy young adult will have a blood pressure reading of 120/80 mm Hg (millimetres of mercury).

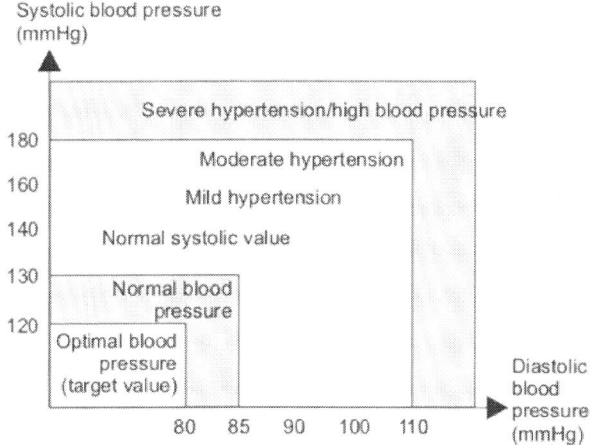

According to the blood pressure classification by the WHO/ISH.

Figure 10 – An illustration of normal and unhealthy blood pressure levels.

See also – Blood; Blood vessels; Cardiovascular system; Heart; Hypertension.

ABC GUIDE TO ANATOMY AND PHYSIOLOGY

Body temperature maintenance

Normal body temperature for human beings is between 36.5 and 37.5 C. A person's body temperature must be maintained within this narrow range to ensure optimum health and functioning.

Thermoregulation, or body temperature control, is maintained through a negative feedback system in which changes in temperature are detected and corrective action is taken to keep core body temperature constant. This is vital to prevent the body's internal organs from overheating. The body will respond to:

- hot conditions by losing heat to keep the core cool
- cold conditions by retaining heat to keep the core warm

Temperature receptors in the skin and around internal organs pick up and report changes in temperature to the brain. The brain then switches on either the body's heat loss or heat retention mechanisms in response to this.

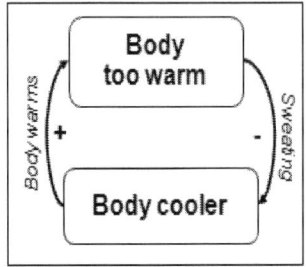 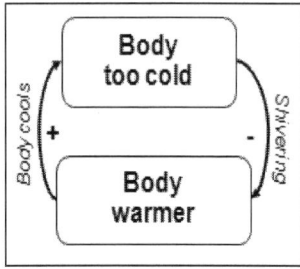

Figure 11 – The body will respond to external conditions in order to ensure internal, core, temperature is kept within normal limits.

See also – Homeostasis; Homeostatic failure; Negative feedback

Bone

Bone is a specialised connective tissue. It consists of special cells called osteoblasts and osteoclasts as well as a matrix embedded with fibres. Many bones also have a central cavity that contains marrow. Bone marrow tissue is the source of most blood cells. The extracellular matrix that bones are made of gradually becomes calcified during childhood and adolescence, giving bone its characteristic hardness.

The function of bones is to:

- provide internal support for the body and sites for tendons and muscles to attach to
- protect vital organs around the body
- store calcium and phosphate

There are 206 individual bones in the human body. These include:

- Long bones that allow movement (e.g the femur (thigh) bone, the clavicle (collar) bone and the metatarsals (foot bones).
- Short bones in parts of the body where little movement is required (e.g tarsal (ankle) and carpal (wrist) bones.
- Flat bones that have broad flat surfaces for muscle attachment (e.g the scapula (shoulder) bone, the sternum (breastbone) and the ribs).
- Irregular bones that don't fit any of the above characteristics such as vertebrae, the mandible (lower jaw)and temporal bones (face and head bones)
- Sesamoid bones with tendons. The two main examples are the patella (kneecap) and the hyoid (base of the tongue).

Bone tissue is formed continually throughout life, though bones stop growing in length between the ages of 16 and 18. Despite this, bone density continues to increase until a person's late 20's.

ABC GUIDE TO ANATOMY AND PHYSIOLOGY

Calcium and protein are gradually lost from the bones from about 35 years of age. Post-menopausal women lose bone density much more rapidly in the few years after their menstrual cycle ends. This process can continue into later adulthood, resulting in people becoming physically frail and experiencing more falls and fractures.

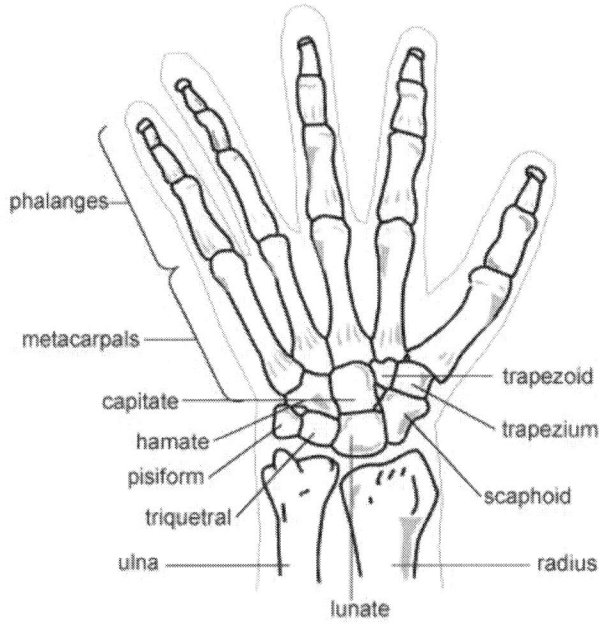

BONES OF THE HAND

Figure 12

See also – Fractures; Joints; Osteoarthritis; Osteoporosis; Skeletal system.

HEALTH AND SOCIAL CARE

Brain

The brain is a highly complex organ located in the cranium (skull) that plays a central part in controlling the body and mind. The three main sections of the brain are the:

- cerebrum (the cerebral hemispheres)
- cerebellum
- brain stem

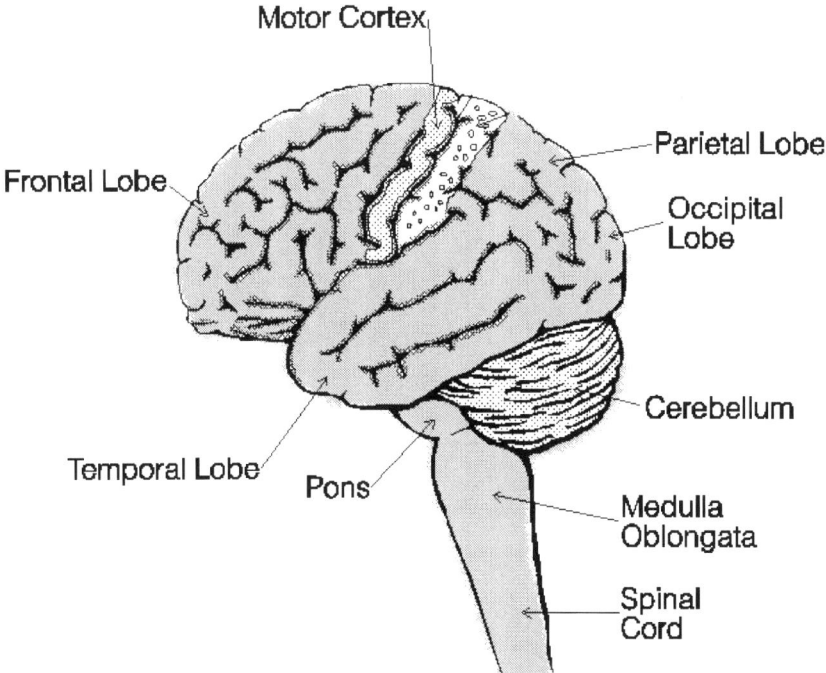

Figure 13 – An illustration of the structure of the human brain.

The cerebrum

The cerebrum is the largest part of the brain. It is divided into the left and right cerebral hemisphere which are sub-divided into a number of lobes (frontal lobe, parietal lobe, temporal lobe, occipital lobe).

The outer layer is made of folds of grey matter (consisting of cell bodies). Inside this is the white matter (consisting of nerve cells and fibres). The white matter fibres of the cerebrum connect various parts of the brain together. Overall, the function of the cerebrum is to:

- control voluntary movement
- identify and interpret conscious sensations (heat, cold, pain)
- control a range of mental activities (memory, reasoning, intelligence)

The cerebellum

This part of the brain is located underneath the cerebrum in what is known as the posterior cranial fossa. It has two hemispheres, each with grey matter on the surface and white matter inside. The function of the cerebellum is to:

- coordinate muscle activity, ensuring smooth, precise movement
- subconsciously control and maintain muscle tone and posture
- maintain the balance and equilibrium of the body.

The brain stem

This part of the brain is made up of three parts: the midbrain; the pons Varolii and the medulla oblongata.

As the name implies, the midbrain sits between the cerebrum and the cerebellum and above the pons Varolii . It is only about 2cm long, consisting of nerve cells and fibres. It is the part of the brain that transmits messages to and from the spinal cord, the cerebrum and the cerebellum.

HEALTH AND SOCIAL CARE

The pons Varolii is located in front of the cerebellum, below the midbrain and above the medulla oblongata. It is made up of nerve cells that link the two hemispheres of the cerebellum. Its main function is to transmit messages to and from the cerebrum and spinal cord.

The medulla oblongata is the lowest part of the brainstem., located above the spinal cord and below the pons Varolii. Unusually, it has white matter on the surface and grey matter in the centre. It controls the action of the heart and lungs as well as the constriction and dilation of blood vessels and the body's reflex actions (vomiting, coughing, sneezing, swallowing).

See also – Central nervous system; Dementia; Muscular system; Nervous tissue; Parkinson's disease; Stroke

ABC GUIDE TO ANATOMY AND PHYSIOLOGY

Cardiovascular system

The cardiovascular system consists of the heart, the blood and blood vessels (arteries, veins and capillaries).

In basic terms, the cardiovascular system is a pumping system. The cardiovascular system's function is to move substances around the body. The main substances it moves are the respiratory gases (carbon dioxide and oxygen) and food (nutrients) using blood as the transport medium.

Figure 14 – Substances carried by the blood

Substance	Moved from	Moved to	Why?
Oxygen	Lungs	Every cell in the body	For use in respiration
Carbon dioxide	Every cell in the body	The lungs	Passed out in exhaled air.
Food substances	The gut	Every cell in the body	Used for energy or to nourish the body.
Hormones	Endocrine gland	Target organs	To control body organs
Urea	The liver	The kidneys	Excreted in the urine.
Antibodies	Lymph glands	Infected areas	Protect against disease
Heat	Hotter areas	Cooler areas	To equalise temperature in the body

See also – Autonomic nervous system; Blood; Blood vessels; Heart; Respiratory system

Catabolism

Catabolism is the chemical process of breaking down molecules that occurs in body cells to release energy.

Catabolism breaks down organic matter to harvest energy in cellular respiration and is sometimes referred to as 'destructive metabolism'. Cells break down large molecules (fats and carbohydrates usually) to release energy. This release of energy provides fuel for anabolism, heats the body and enables the muscles to contract and the body to move.

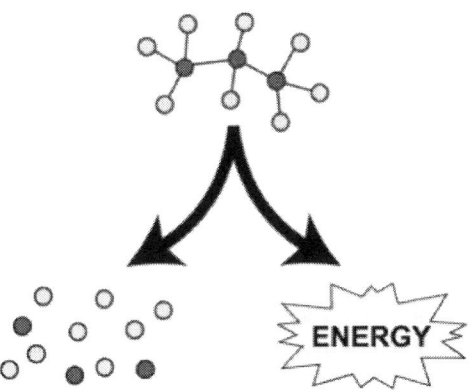

Figure 15 – Catabolism is a process of molecular destruction that leads to the release of energy.

See also – Anabolism; Cells; Energy metabolism; Energy transformation.

ABC GUIDE TO ANATOMY AND PHYSIOLOGY

Cells

A cell is the smallest unit of living matter that can reproduce itself.

There are about 50 trillion (50 million million) cells in the human body. These cells are very active and are essential for life. It may come as a surprise to know that you began life as a clump of just eight very special stem cells. These eight cells made up the human embryo from which you developed. Each of the stem cells had the potential to develop into any of the different cells that make up your body. Over time they divided and differentiated into specialist cells types – nerve, bone and muscle cells, for example – each with a specific function.

The function of human cells is to live and sustain life! Cells are the basic structure of the human body. Groups of cells form tissues, organs and body fluids. The functions of cells include:

- respiration – oxygen is absorbed and energy and carbon dioxide produced as a result of respiration processes in the cell
- sensitivity – cells respond to a variety of mechanical, electrical, thermal and chemical stimuli
- growth – cells grow and repair by making protein
- reproduction – cells grow to maturity and then reproduce themselves via mitosis (cell division) or meiosis (sexual reproduction)
- excretion – waste that is harmful to cells (carbon dioxide, urea) is removed
- metabolism – chemical reactions required to make proteins (for growth / repair) or to breakdown substances and produce energy occur in the cell.

HEALTH AND SOCIAL CARE

When cells misfunction and are not replaced or repaired, the body goes wrong. Cell failure or misfunctioning is the foundation of many diseases and illness conditions.

Figure 16 – Different types of cell

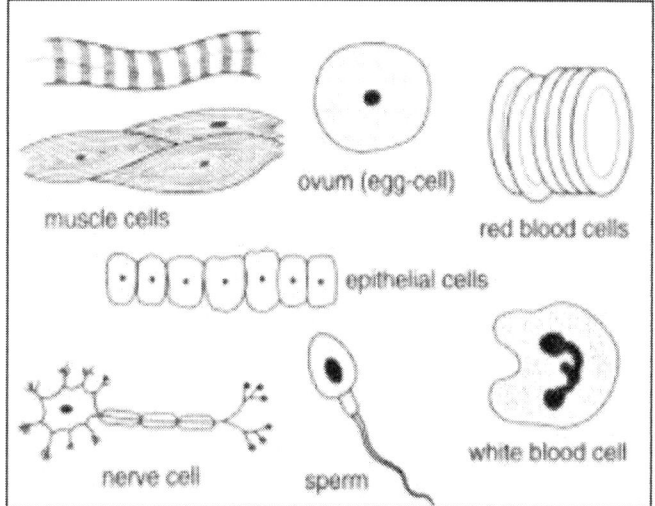

Different types of cell

See also –Anabolism; Catabolism; Cell structure; Conception; Energy metabolism.

ABC GUIDE TO ANATOMY AND PHYSIOLOGY

Cell structure

Cells are the smallest, microscopic elements of the body. Each cell has three parts:

- a nucleus that controls the way the cells works – as a nerve cell, a muscle cell or a blood cell, for example
- cytoplasm, a jelly-like substance containing the structures that enable the cell to function
- a membrane surrounding and protecting the cell

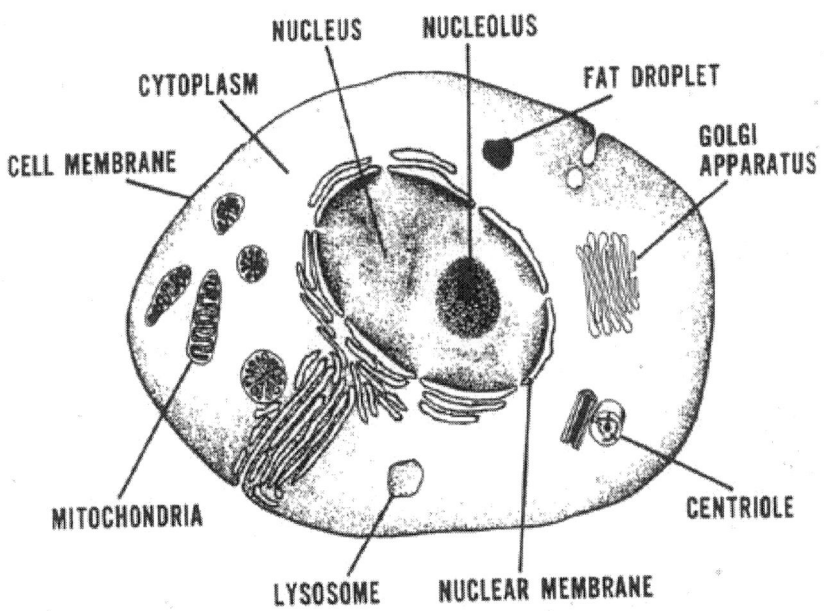

Figure 17 – The structure of a basic human cell

The nucleus
The nucleus is the largest structure in a cell. There is usually only one nucleus in each cell, though there are also a number of types of cell that have more than one nucleus (e.g muscle cells) and some red blood cells and bacterial cells have no nucleus at all. In general, the nucleus is spherical in shape, contains the cells DNA and can be found in the centre of the cell. The nucleus is surrounded by a porous plasma membrane that allows proteins and nucleic acids to pass through. The nucleus is the control centre of the cell, controlling all of its functions.

Cytoplasm
Cytoplasm is the gel-like substance found between the outer boundary and the membrane surrounding the nucleus in a cell. It is where various chemical reactions, or the metabolism, of the cell occur. Cytoplasm contains a complex mix of enzymes, sugars such as glycogen and melanin and waste materials.

Cell organelles
The cell organelles are the various structures within a cell each have their own function. In some ways they are like mini-versions of the organs of the human body – hence the term organelles. Key organelles include:

- mitochondria
- the endoplasmic reticulum
- the Golgi apparatus
- lysosomes

Mitochondria

These are relatively large, individual organelles that appear in large numbers in most body cells. They are usually sausage-like or spherical in shape. Their function is to make ATP through aerobic respiration. ATP is a molecule that provides chemical energy to cell processes that require it. Mitochondria have an unusual double membrane structure: a smooth outer layer and a folded inner layer. The large internal surface of the inner layer enables the complex aerobic respiration process to take place.

The endoplasmic reticulum

Endoplasmic reticulum (ER) is a system of complex tunnels or channels spread throughout the cell. The outside surface of the ER is known as 'rough ER'. This is because it has ribosomes attached to it, giving it a studded or grainy appearance under a microscope. The function of the rough ER is to collect together and transport proteins made on the ribosomes. The second type of ER is known as 'smooth ER'. This doesn't have any ribosomes attached to it and is responsible for steroid (lipid hormone) production. It is also a storage site for calcium in skeletal muscle cells and contains enzymes that detoxify a variety of organic molecules.

The Golgi apparatus

This is a tightly packed group of flattened, fluid-filled cavities or vesicles that shift and change as vesicles are added and lost. The Golgi apparatus is thought to play an important role in synthesising and modifying proteins, lipids and carbohydrates. Proteins made on the ribosomes attached to the ER are packaged into vesicles that then join with the Golgi apparatus to be modified and secreted out of the cell or into lysomes.

Lysomes

These are best describes as bags of digestive enzymes. They are found in cell cytoplasm and in small vesicles produced by the Golgi apparatus. They contain powerful lytic enzymes that can:

HEALTH AND SOCIAL CARE

- destroy old or surplus organelles in a cell
- digest material taken into a cell – such as bacterium or carbon particles
- destroy whole cells and tissues that are no longer required (e.g the muscle of the uterus after giving birth and milk-producing tissue after breast feeding finishes)

See also –Anabolism; Catabolism; Cells; Conception; Energy metabolism; Sickle cell disease; Tissues.

ABC GUIDE TO ANATOMY AND PHYSIOLOGY

Central nervous system

The central nervous system or CNS includes the brain and spinal cord. The brain contains two main types of tissue:

- grey matter which is made up of the cell bodies of nerve cells.
- white matter which includes all the fibres running between nerve cells and other organs

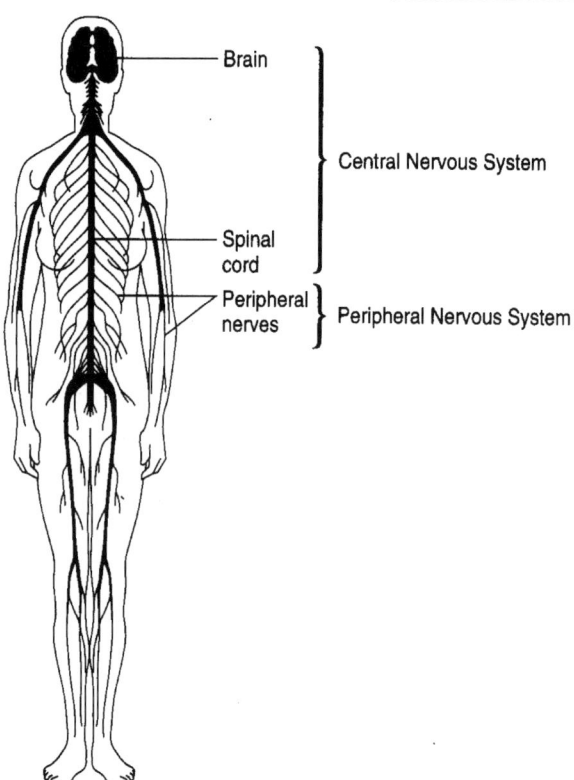

Figure 18 – The central nervous system is composed of the brain and the spinal cord.

HEALTH AND SOCIAL CARE

The grey matter in the brain covers the outer surface and has the job of 'thinking' – it is our grey matter that makes us 'smart'. Different parts of the brain do different jobs but they all depend on good connections. These connections are the nerve fibres. They carry nerve impulses across the nervous system. Each fibre is insulated from the ones next to it by a thin covering of myelin. It is the myelin that makes the white matter look white.

The spinal cord is the other important part of the central nervous system. It begins at the medulla oblongata in the brain and extends through the spinal vertebrae to the first lumbar vertebrae at the base of the spine. It has white matter on the surface and grey matter inside (opposite to the brain) and branches into 31 pairs of spinal nerves and part of one crania nerve. The function of the spinal cord is to carry motor and sensory nerve fibres, sending messages between the body and the brain.

See also – Autonomic nervous system; Brain; Multiple sclerosis; Nervous tissue; Parkinson's disease; Stroke

ABC GUIDE TO ANATOMY AND PHYSIOLOGY

Chorionic villi sampling (CVS)

Chorionic villi sampling is a screening test that is used to identify genetic abnormalities in a developing foetus. Pregnant women are only offered this test – between 11 and 14 weeks into their pregnancy – if there is a high risk that their baby may have a genetic condition.

Under ultrasound guidance, a long thin needle is inserted through the woman's abdomen into the placenta. A small sample of cells are then removed from the chorionic villi and tested for chromosomal abnormalities. The results are usually available a few days later. CVS has a higher risk of miscarriage (1-2%) than amniocentesis (1%) but can be carried out earlier and allows chromosomal diagnosis as well as gene sampling.

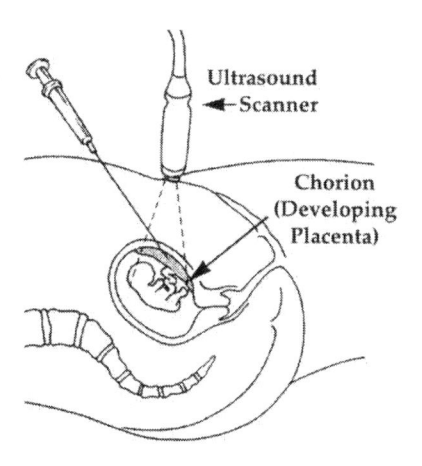

Figure 19 – An illustration of the CVS process.

See also – Amniocentesis; Conception; Cystic fibrosis; Down's syndrome; Foetal development;

Coronary Heart Disease (CHD)

Coronary heart disease (CHD) is the consequence of an interrupted or blocked blood supply to the heart. It is typically caused by fatty substances building up, narrowing and ultimately blocking the coronary arteries. CHD is one of the major causes of death in the richer countries of the world.

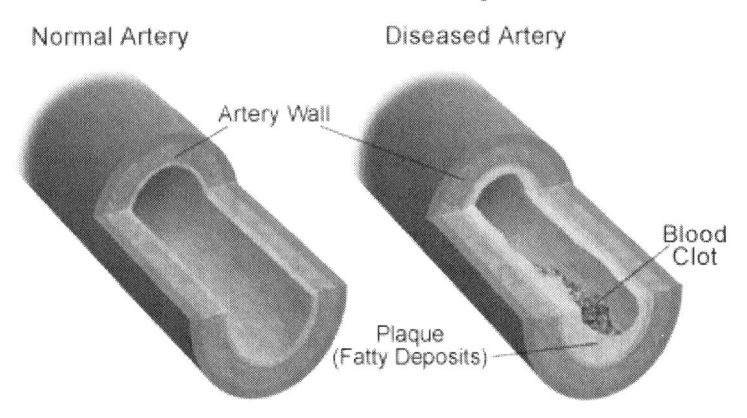

Figure 20 – A build-up of fatty deposits in the arteries supplying the heart cause CHD.

Like every other muscle in the body, the heart needs a constant supply of food and oxygen and to get rid of carbon dioxide. The blood flowing through the heart cannot do this efficiently enough so the muscles of the heart have their own blood supply. The coronary artery delivers fresh, oxygenated blood to the muscles of the ventricles. Any blockage in the coronary artery will starve the heart muscle of blood and lead to serious damage – possibly even death.

Cholesterol is a fatty substance that is needed by the body to build cells and nerves. However, if our diet is too high in fats, particularly animal fats, the concentration of the cholesterol in the blood rises above a safe level. This encourages the formation of fatty deposits called plaques on the inside walls of arteries. These plaques slowly close down the space in the artery where the blood flows – effectively the artery furs up with fat. This process is known as atherosclerosis. When this happens in the coronary artery, it cannot carry enough blood to the heart muscles.

Factors that make CHD more likely are:

- A high-fat diet (particularly animal fats)
- Lack of exercise
- Being overweight
- Smoking
- Stress
- Genetic factors – some people seem to inherit a greater chance of suffering from CHD from their parents.

The good news on CHD is that almost all of the risk factors are under our control – we can choose to eat a healthier diet, take more exercise and, if we smoke – we should stop. Even stress responds well to being healthy – people who have a good diet, plenty of exercise and look after themselves seem to cope much better with stress than people who are overweight and unfit.

See also - Cardiovascular system; Blood vessels; Heart; Hypertension; stroke

Chronic obstructive pulmonary disease (COPD)

Chronic obstructive pulmonary disease is a progressive disorder that affects the respiratory system and a person's ability to breathe freely.

People who are diagnosed with COPD usually have emphysema and/or chronic bronchitis. Emphysema is characterised by damage to the walls of many of the air sacs (alveoli) that cause them to lose their shape and become floppy. In some cases, the walls of the air sacs are destroyed, leading to fewer, larger air sacs instead of many tiny ones. This reduces the surface area for gaseous exchange in the lungs. Chronic bronchitis is characterised by constantly inflamed and irritated airways. The lining of the airways thickens and thick mucus is produced in the airways making airflow and breathing more difficult.

The symptoms of COPD include coughing that produces large amounts of slimy mucus, wheezing and shortness of breath and chest tightness. The main cause of COPD is cigarette smoking. Exposure, usually over a long period, to other lung irritants (air pollution, chemical fumes or dust) may also lead to COPD. The condition is not infectious and cannot be passed on genetically. Stopping smoking, avoiding sources of lung irritants as much as possible, medication and oxygen therapy (delivered through portable oxygen tanks at home) can slow the progress of the condition but cannot stop the irreversible process of declining lung function.

Many people are disabled by the symptoms of COPD, which get worse over time as the condition slowly progresses. As people become more disabled by their breathing difficulties they tend to have to give up work and other life roles and struggle with basic activities such as walking, cooking and self-care (Dressing / washing). Most people with COPD will die as a result of the condition they have. Overall, it is a major cause of death in the United Kingdom.

See also – Lungs; Gaseous exchange; Respiratory system.

Clinical trial

A clinical trial is a way of carrying out health care-related research. Generally, it involves comparing one treatment or health care intervention with another.

Comparison of treatment and non-treatment groups within a research population are an important feature of clinical trials. As a result, clinical trials can include patients (people with a confirmed diagnosis), healthy people and/or both. A clinical trial may initially be based on a small number of participants to test a hypothesis. The trial may then be extended and carried out on a much larger number of people to produce results that are much more reliable.

Clinical trials, particularly randomized control trials (RCTs), play an important part in the development of medical science and healthcare practice. In particular, they provide healthcare practitioners and patients with evidence about the effectiveness of specific treatments, procedures or approaches to clinical practice. This can include identifying the side-effects of treatments and allows clinicians to assess whether a new treatment or approach is better than the established or standard one. Research data that informs clinical decision-making and evidence-based practice reduces the risk of harmful or ineffective treatments being used and prevents wastage of NHS resources.

See also – Epidemiological study; Morbidity; Mortality.

Coeliac disease

Coeliac disease is a digestive condition caused by an adverse reaction to the gluten protein. Gluten is found in foods such as bread, cereals, pasta and biscuits that contain wheat flour.

Coeliac disease is an auto-immune condition in which the immune system reacts against gliadin (a component of gluten protein) which it sees as a virus-like threat to the body. The antibodies produced by the immune system to neutralise gliadin cause inflammation to the surface of the intestine. This prevents the intestine from digesting the nutrients in food and causes a range of other uncomfortable and sometimes painful physical symptoms. These include cramping, bloating, flatulence, weight loss, diarrhoea, tiredness and fatigue, tingling in the hands and feet and swelling in a person's hands, feet and limbs due to fluid build-up. A person with coeliac disease may also become malnourished and may develop conditions such as anaemia and osteoporosis because their body is unable to absorb sufficient nutrients in food or because they have been avoiding eating to reduce their symptoms.

Coeliac disease is diagnosed through a blood test (to identify antibodies in the blood) and a biopsy of the small intestine. A small amount of the small intestine lining is taken and then analysed for signs of Coeliac disease. A person diagnosed with Coeliac disease will be told to exclude food containing gluten from their diet. Many everyday foods such as meat, vegetables, rice, cheese and potatoes do not contain gluten and can still be eaten. However, foods containing wheat, rye, barley and spelt flour must be avoided to prevent a return of symptoms.

See also – Alimentary canal; Intestines; Digestion; Digestive system; Ileum; Stomach

Conception

In biological terms, human life begins with the process of conception. Both the male and female reproductive systems need to be functioning effectively for conception to take place.

The female sex hormones oestrogen and progesterone are produced by the ovaries and control the female menstrual cycle. An average menstrual cycle lasts 28 days. During the first part of the cycle, the lining of the uterus (womb) thickens. Around day 14 of the cycle a female ovum (egg) is released from the ovary into the fallopian tube, a process called ovulation. If the ovum is not fertilised by a male sperm, then it will be expelled with the lining of the uterus as a menstrual bleed.

The testes produce the male sex hormone testosterone, which stimulates sperm production. Sperm are made in the testes and stored in the epididymis. The sperm mix with semen from the seminal vesicle and are ejected from the penis in an ejaculation. During sexual intercourse, sperm are deposited in the vagina and swim up through the female reproductive system to reach the fallopian tubes.

After ovulation, the ripe ovum travels along the fallopian tube to the uterus. This journey usually takes five to seven days. If sexual intercourse takes place during this time, the egg may become fertilised by a male sperm in the fallopian tube. The fertilised ovum will then attach itself to the wall of the uterus. The fertilised egg will then start to develop into an embryo and begin to grow rapidly. The growth and development of the baby in the uterus (womb) usually takes place over 37 to 42 weeks (full-term pregnancy) and can be divided into three different phases known as trimesters.

See also – Cells; Cell structure; Foetal development; Reproductive system.

Connective tissue

Connective tissues connect body structures together and can be found throughout the human body (see figure 19). All connective tissues except blood have a structural role in the body.

Figure 21 – Main types of connective tissue

Tissue type	Function
Bone	Forms the skeleton, protects and supports body organs and anchors muscles.
Cartilage	Smoothes surfaces at joints, prevents collapse of trachea and bronchi.
Adipose	Stores fat and insulates the body.
Blood	Transports substances around the body.
Areolar	Protects organs, blood vessels and nerves and strengthens epithelial tissue.

Unlike epithelial cells, connective tissue cells are not packed closely together. Instead, they are separated by a non-cellular matrix (a mesh) whose composition gives each type of connective tissue its particular characteristics.

See also – Blood; Bone; Cell structure; Tissue;

Cystic fibrosis

Cystic fibrosis (CF) is an inherited condition that affects the lungs and digestive system.

CF is one of the commonest genetic diseases in the UK with roughly 1 in 2500 babies born with the illness. A damaged gene that stops people who carry it from controlling the movement of salt into and out of their body cells properly causes CF. This has effects on the lungs, pancreas and lower gut particularly but can lead to problems all over the body.

In the lungs, the mucus that normally protects the internal surfaces becomes quite thick and sticky. This makes it difficult to move so it clogs up the small tubes and can act as a reservoir for infection. A child with CF often suffers from repeated chest infections that make them weak and slow their growth. Damage to the pancreas can affect appetite and can lead to *diabetes mellitus*. Again, this can lead to slow growth and a general 'unwellness'.

Recently, new treatments have improved the health of people with CF enormously. A high-calorie diet with added vitamins (A, D, E and K) and a package of enzymes helps growth. Antibiotics can now also keep lung infections under control. Recent clinical trials have also used genetic engineering techniques to insert undamaged genes into the cells of the lung lining. These genes 'teach' the cells how to control salt movement across the cell membranes. This reduces the thickness of the mucus and so helps to prevent build-up of infection. In the future this may provide a cure for CF.

See also –Digestive system; Lungs; Mendelian Inheritance Principles; Respiratory system;

Dementia

Dementia is a general term that is used to describe (or categorise) a range of different medical conditions that affect the structure and functioning of the human brain. This means that there is no condition that is simply called 'dementia'. Instead, 'dementia' is a term used to describe a set of symptoms (a syndrome) caused by a number of different diseases. Perhaps the most well-known of these diseases is Alzheimer's disease. Other examples of condition that cause dementia symptoms include vascular dementia, frontotemporal dementia and dementia with Lewy bodies.

Brian Draper, a professor and consultant psychiatrist specialising in old age psychiatry, defines dementia as 'an acquired decline in memory and thinking (cognition) due to brain disease that results in significant impairment of personal, social or occupational function' (2013: 13). The changes that occur in a person's brain typically lead to:

- death of nerve cells or loss of communication between nerve cells in the brain
- multiple cognitive deficits, including memory impairment
- problems with using language
- failure to recognise people
- problems in orientation – knowing what time of day or year it is and where the person is
- decline in overall mental functioning.

Most dementia-related conditions develop gradually but are progressive and irreversible. This isn't quite the same as saying the symptoms of dementia can't be treated or that the course of a person's condition or the rate of their decline can't be influenced. Many people are able to 'live well' with dementia for a period of time and can maintain and experience a good quality of life with adaptations to and support within their everyday living environment.

Diagnosing 'dementia'

Initially, and sometimes with hindsight, a person may be aware that their short-term memory (ability to remember recent events) has got worse. This might provoke – or be accompanied by – anxiety and depression, personality and behaviour changes (especially apathy and irritability) and difficulties in personal and/or work relationships as the person becomes less able to cope with the demands of their everyday life. A person's dementia-based condition is often not diagnosed at this stage as the individual, their family members, employer and even the medical professionals they see, may view their problems as being the result of 'stress', anxiety or depression or even 'just part of old age'. When treatment or support for these things fail to resolve the person's problems or their short-term memory, confusion and disorientation continue to worsen, further cognitive or neuropsychological tests and brain scans tend to be carried out. These aim to identify whether, and if so how, the person's brain and cognitive functioning have changed. It is usually at this point that a person is diagnosed with a form of 'dementia'.

See also – Brain; Central Nervous System;

Diabetes

Diabetes is a condition in which the body is unable to control blood sugar levels due to its inability to produce or make effective use of the hormone insulin.

Diabetes insipidus (Type 2)
A person's body may not respond appropriately to the insulin that their pancreas is actually producing. As a result, glucose stays in the person's blood, raising their blood glucose levels rather than being moved into the person's cells to produce energy. Diabetes insipidus is more commonly known as Type 2 diabetes but may also be called 'insulin-resistant' or 'adult-onset diabetes'. It is most likely to occur because of excess weight and lack of exercise. Genetic factors also play a part too. A person who has a relative with Type 2 diabetes has a greater risk of developing the condition themselves – the closer the relative (e.g parent or sibling), the greater the risk.

Diabetes mellitus (Type 1)
About 2% of people in Britain suffer from *diabetes mellitus* ('sugar diabetes'). They cannot produce enough insulin and so their blood glucose level can rise above the safe level. To try to prevent this happening they try to avoid sugary foods and may inject insulin when they know their blood glucose is rising. Insulin is usually injected 2 to 4 times a day and meals and snacks are carefully planned to keep blood sugar within safe limits. The diabetic has to *consciously* do some of the work that the pancreas does automatically in a person without the disease.

Sometimes the control goes wrong. Maybe the person injected a little too much insulin, or the meal was delayed, or some unexpected physical activity used up the store of sugar in the blood. All of these things drive the blood sugar down below the safe level and a hypoglycaemic coma or 'hypo' can occur. 'Hypo' means 'too low' and 'glycaemic' means 'glucose in the blood' so a hypoglycaemic coma is produced by a blood glucose level that is too low. The person feels sweaty, pale, possibly aggressive and can fall into a coma. A coma is a sudden, deep sleep that the person does not wake easily from. A diabetic in a hypo should be given some sugary food or drink immediately – even a teaspoonful of jam or honey will help - to boost their blood sugar.

Fortunately, sugar can be absorbed directly through the lining of the mouth. This usually leads to a quick recovery.

A hyperglycaemic coma is caused when the level of glucose in the blood has been too high for a few days. 'Hyper' means 'too high'. The high levels of glucose mean the person excretes a lot of urine and can become dehydrated. The dehydration is very dangerous and can cause a sudden collapse and a coma. Diabetics who go into a hyperglycaemic coma usually need hospital treatment before they recover.

See also – Blood; Blood glucose levels; Endocrine system; Homeostasis; Homeostatic failure

ABC GUIDE TO ANATOMY AND PHYSIOLOGY

Digestion

Digestion is the process of breaking down food into substances that can be absorbed and assimilated by the human body.

The process of digestion begins when food is first ingested, or taken into, the mouth. It is then chewed by the tongue and teeth and softened by saliva. This starts to break the food down. A small ball of food called a bolus is then created and swallowed. This first stage of the digestive process is known as mechanical digestion.

Once mechanical digestion is completed, the food ball goes down the oesophagus, partly through gravity and partly through a process called peristalsis, to the stomach. When the food reaches the stomach, chemical digestion takes place as it is broken down further by enzymes and gastric juices. This partly digested food stays in the stomach for about five hours. It is then pushed into the small intestine for further chemical digestion. More enzymes and pancreatic juices then break the food down into the components that the body needs and can absorb. This process takes about four hours. Between seven and nine hours after food has first been eaten, it will have reached a stage where the nutrients have been extracted and the remaining undigested mass is moved into the large intestine as faeces. This will now be eliminated via the anus.

See also – Alimentary canal; Digestive system; Energy transformation; Ileum; Intestines; Stomach.

Digestive system

The digestive system is responsible for the physical and chemical digestion, absorption and elimination of food materials. The process of digestion involves a number of different body structures, each with their own particular digestive function.

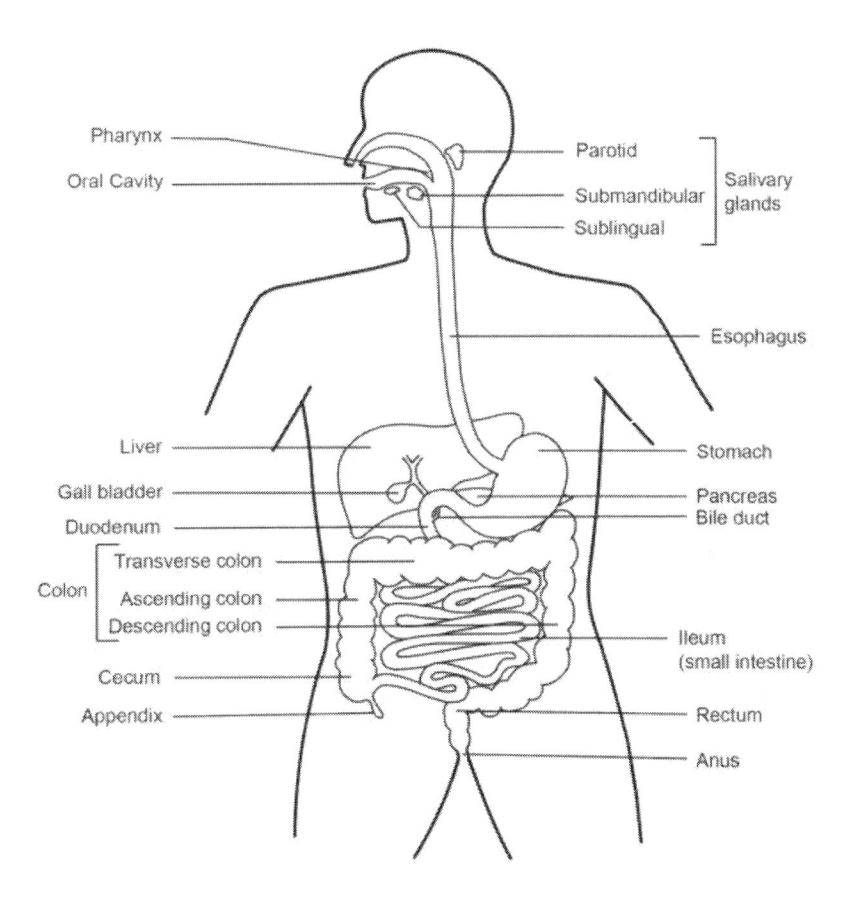

Figure 22 – The digestive system involves a number of different body structures.

ABC GUIDE TO ANATOMY AND PHYSIOLOGY

The salivary glands
There are three pairs of salivary glands in the oral cavity. Between them these glands secrete between 1 and 1.5 litres of saliva per day. There are two types of saliva. The purpose of the thin, watery type of saliva is to wet food. This is done by the tongue during chewing. The second thick, mucous-like secretion lubricates and causes food particles to stick together and form the bolus that is swallowed. As well as lubricating food and cleaning the mouth, saliva also begins the chemical breakdown of food because it contains a digestive enzyme called salivary amylase

The oesophagus
This is a narrow, muscular tube about 20-30 centimetres in length which begins at the back of the mouth and transports the bolus of food down to the stomach. It takes about 7 seconds for food to get from your mouth to your stomach via the oesophagus. The external wall of the oesophagus consists of two layers of smooth muscle which contract (peristalsis) to move the food along. At the top of the oesophagus is a flap of tissue called the epiglottis. This closes when you swallow to prevent food from entering your trachea (windpipe). No digestion actually takes place in the oesophagus because no enzymes are released here.

The stomach
Your stomach is a relatively small pouch made of thick elastic muscles. It is mainly located behind your rib cage and under the diaphragm. The purpose of the stomach is to store and help break down food. Once it has entered from the oesophagus, food can remain in the stomach for up to three hours. It is churned by the stomach walls to break it down into smaller pieces and also covered in gastric acid, pepsin and other digestive enzymes to form a semi-liquid solution known as chyme. This is then moved on for further digestion in the small intestine

The duodenum

The small intestine is surprisingly long at about 6 metres in length. It is quite small in diameter though, hence its name. The duodenum is the first, shorter section of the small intestine. It is where the milky chyme enters the duodenum and where most digestion and absorption takes place. Once the chyme enters the duodenum it is mixed with bile from the liver and gall bladder and pancreatic juice made by the pancreas. The walls of the duodenum also secrete intestinal enzymes that break down proteins, carbohydrates and fats (lipids). The partly digested chyme now moves further down the alimentary canal into the ileum.

The ileum

The function of the ileum is the absorption of the fully digested food into the circulatory and lymphatic systems. The ileum contains small finger-like structures called villi that are themselves covered in hair-like microvilli that provide a very large surface area for the absorption of nutrients. Absorbed nutrients are carried in the blood to the liver where the blood is filtered to remove toxins and where the nutrients are processed further. Meanwhile, the food mass from which the nutrients have been extracted is now moved via peristalsis into the colon.

The colon

The colon, along with the rectum, is part of the large intestine. The colon is about 1.5 metres long. It runs up the right side of the abdomen (ascending colon), goes across the body (traverse colon) and then down the left side of the abdomen (descending colon) until it ends at the anus where faeces is expelled. No enzymes are secreted in the large intestine though some absorption of fluid and nutrients does take place. The large intestine absorbs water from the food bolus and stores faeces until it can be excreted. Stored faeces are eliminated from the body through contraction and relaxation of the anus. The biological term for passing this waste material out of the body is egestion.

The liver
The liver is the largest internal organ in the human body. It is on the right side of the abdominal cavity just below the diaphragm and overlapping the stomach. The liver performs a number of functions including:
- storing iron and some vitamins
- removing drugs and alcohol from the blood
- helping to control levels of glucose in the blood
- producing heat that keeps the body warm
- producing bile salts that break down fat in the small intestines.

Bile passes into the duodenum via the bile duct. It emulsifies fats to form tiny globules that can be further broken down by enzymes.

The pancreas
The pancreas is positioned between the intestine and stomach, close to the duodenum. The function of the pancreas is to produce hormones that control glucose levels in the blood and to secrete enzymes into the small intestine to help the body to break down and digest food.

Peristalsis
Peristalsis is the term used to describe the slow muscular movements that move food and chyme down the alimentary canal. The alimentary canal has two sheets of smooth muscle – one running down the tube and the other encircling it – that work in an antagonistic way. When the inner circle of muscle contracts behind the bolus of food or chyme the muscle running length ways relaxes. This has the effect of pushing the material forward. Slow, rhythmic repetitions of this process gradually move the food or chyme through the alimentary canal.

Digestive enzymes

Digestive enzymes are produced by the human body to break down complex food molecules such as carbohydrates, proteins and fats into simpler ones. Enzymes act as catalysts. This means that they change the rate of chemical reactions in the cells to allow the breakdown or build-up of other chemicals without being changed themselves.

Enzymes have very specific actions. Each enzyme acts on a particular type of material, known as a substrate. Protease only acts on protein, for example, and lipase only acts on fats (lipids). Each enzyme:

- is produced in a specific part of the body (site of production)
- has a particular site of activity where it promotes chemical digestion
- requires surroundings with a particular acidity or alkalinity (pH) to work effectively
- acts on a particular food component (substrate)
- produces a particular chemical component of food (products) that can be used by the body

See also – Alimentary canal; Digestion; Ileum; Intestines; Stomach

Down's syndrome

Down's syndrome is a genetic disorder caused by a randomly occurring (and not inherited) chromosomal abnormality that affects 1 in 1000 UK babies. Specifically, a person with Down's syndrome has all or part of an additional chromosome 21. As a result, Down's syndrome is also sometimes referred to as Trisomy 21.

Pregnant women are screened for Down's syndrome during pregnancy. A blood test and ultrasound scan (the combined test) is typically offered between week 10 and 14 of a woman's pregnancy. This assesses the likelihood of the woman having a baby with Down's syndrome. Other blood tests can also be carried out later in the pregnancy. If there is a high risk of Down's syndrome, an amniocentesis or chorionic villus sampling (CVS) procedure may be offered to diagnose whether the developing foetus does have Down's syndrome. Overall, the risk of having a child with Down's syndrome increases with the mother's age.

Down's syndrome affects physical growth and development as well as intellectual development. The physical characteristics of babies with Down's syndrome include:
- hypotonia (reduced muscle tone / floppiness)
- a small mouth and protruding tongue
- eyes that slant upwards and outwards
- below average height and weight
- a flat back of the head

A person with Down's syndrome will also have delayed physical growth and development and mild to moderate intellectual disabilities caused by a restricted IQ (intelligence) level. Whilst this may affect an individual's ability to live independently and their need for ongoing support and assistance, Down's syndrome doesn't, in itself, prevent a person from living an interesting, useful and fulfilling life.

Supported education and care as well as regular health monitoring are needed by people with Down's syndrome to achieve and maintain a good quality of life. Specialist education, supported work opportunities and sheltered housing are available in the UK for people with Down's syndrome who can benefit from, and want, them. Some people with Down's syndrome do achieve independent living but may also require forms of financial, medical and social support to maintain this.

Life expectancy for a person with Down's syndrome in the UK is shorter than average life expectancy at 50-60 years. A great deal depends on whether a person with Down's syndrome also has a congenital heart defect. Those born without heart problems live longer. In addition to a higher risk of being born with a heart defect, people with Down's syndrome also have higher rates of mental illness, epilepsy and Alzheimer's disease. Visual problems, hearing impairment and chronic ear infections are also common in this group of people.

See also – Amniocentesis; Chorionic villus sampling; Foetal development

ABC GUIDE TO ANATOMY AND PHYSIOLOGY

Endocrine system

The endocrine system is a collection of glands that produce hormones which regulate metabolism, growth and development, tissue function, sexual function, sleep and mood, for example. The major endocrine glands in the human body include the pineal gland, pituitary gland, pancreas, ovaries, testes, thyroid gland, parathyroid gland, hypothalamus, gastrointestinal tract and adrenal glands.

The endocrine and nervous systems work together to control conditions *within* the body and respond to changes *outside* the body. These systems have similar functions and share some structures. However, the way they carry out their tasks is quite different.

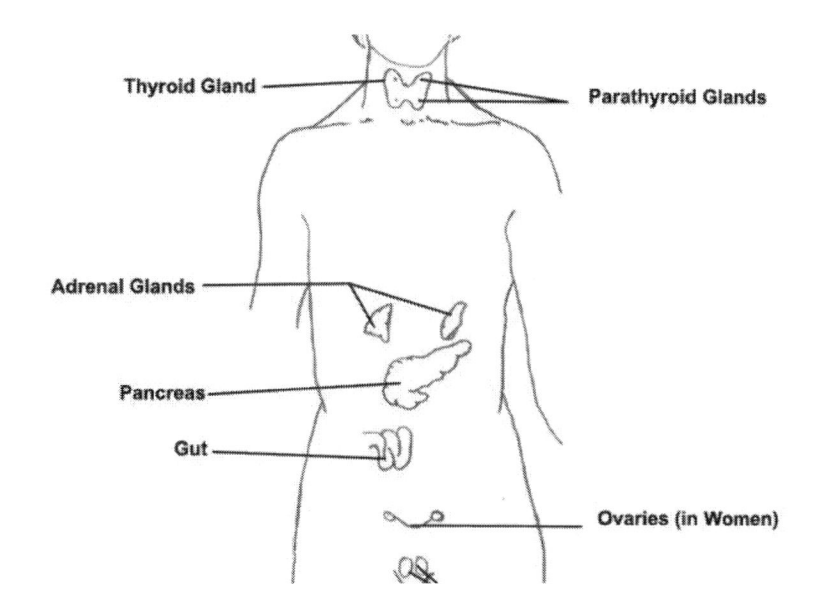

Figure 23 – The location of key endocrine glands in the human body.

HEALTH AND SOCIAL CARE

Different parts of the endocrine system are found all over the body and can work together provided blood flows through both of them.

Hormones are chemicals produced by endocrine glands that travel in the bloodstream to another organ and change the way it works. The organ where the hormone has an effect is called the target organ. For example, anti-diuretic hormone (ADH) is produced by the pituitary gland and changes the way the kidney produces urine. So, the kidney is the target organ.

See also – Blood; Central Nervous System; Diabetes; Negative feedback; Pancreas; Polycystic Ovary Syndrome; Reproductive system

Endometriosis

Endometriosis is a gynecological condition in which tissue that should grow within the uterus (womb), grows outside of it.

Endometrial tissue may be found in the ovaries or fallopian tubes, the lining of the abdomen or in the bowel or bladder in women with endometriosis. The main symptoms of endometriosis are pelvic pain and infertility. Other symptoms include:

- painful or heavy periods
- pain in the lower abdomen, pelvis or lower back
- pain during and after sex
- bleeding between periods
- difficulty getting pregnant
- persistent exhaustion and tiredness
- discomfort when going to the toilet

The severity of a woman's symptoms depends on the location of the endometrial tissue in the body. Many women find out they have endometriosis when they are trying, but failing, to conceive. Most are diagnosed between the ages of 25 and 40 years of age. Diagnosis is made by a gynaecologist following an internal pelvic examination or an ultrasound scan to look for ovarian cysts that may be have been caused by endometriosis and a laparoscopy. This is a surgical procedure in which a tiny camera is inserted into the abdomen (under general anaesthetic) to look for endometrial tissue. A small sample (a biopsy) is surgically removed for further laboratory examination if any is found.

HEALTH AND SOCIAL CARE

The exact cause of endometriosis is not known. A number of theories have been put forward to explain why it occurs, including retrograde menstruation. This is the theory that the womb lining doesn't fully leave some women's bodies during a period and embeds itself into the organs of the pelvis. Treatment of endometriosis involves medication to manage pain, hormone treatment and surgery to remove patches of endometrial tissue that are interfering with fertility.

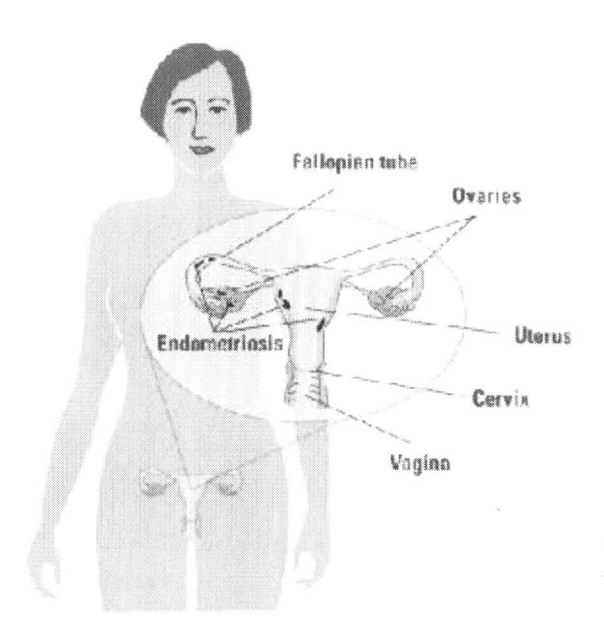

Figure 24 – Common sites of endometriosis.

See also –Conception; Foetal development; Reproductive system; Uterus;

Energy metabolism

One way of understanding the links between energy and the human body is to see your body as a machine that won't work without an energy-rich fuel supply. Food is the source of this energy-rich fuel. But food does not give you energy directly. Firstly, the food you eat must contain the right kinds of materials (nutrients) that can be converted into energy. Then a number of processes have to occur to extract the energy from these materials. This process of converting food into energy is called metabolism.

The process of metabolism illustrates the first law of thermodynamics that says that:

Energy can be transformed from one form to another, but cannot be created or destroyed.

Energy exists in several different forms, including chemical, heat, light, sound and nuclear energy. Chemical energy is the main form of energy used by the human body. Chemical energy is the bond that unites atoms or molecules to each other. When this bond is broken, atoms and the energy in the bond are released.

> ***See also*** – Anabolism; Basal metabolic Rate; catabolism; Energy transformation

Energy transformation

Nothing happens without energy and the body needs a constant supply of energy to stay healthy. The body uses energy to:

- grow – building new tissue requires energy to convert raw materials into the chemicals found in new cells.
- repair – damaged cells need energy to repair the damage.
- move – muscles need a supply of energy for movement, including not just the movements you can see but also the muscles of the heart and the gut inside the body.
- build new chemicals – including the many chemicals made inside the body that you cannot see.
- send nerve impulses – nerve tissue requires a constant supply of energy and dies very quickly if energy is not available.

Yet energy is constantly leaving the body as heat. So, what stops the body from running out of energy rather like a battery in a torch? In biochemical terms the answer is cellular respiration. In other words, if you eat and then metabolise food you will acquire, convert and release the energy needed by your body! This will keep your body's energy levels topped up and will keep you alive. To summarise the situation – *nothing* happens in your body without a supply of energy and that energy *always* comes from your food.

See also – Anabolism; Catabolism; Energy metabolism;

Epidemiological study

An epidemiological study is a systematic investigation and analysis of the patterns, causes and effects of disease, illness (morbidity), death (mortality) and health experiences within a defined population.

Epidemiologists are carry out studies, data analysis and research to explain:

- patterns and variations in rates of illnesses and deaths in populations, specific social groups and geographical localities according to gender, social class, ethnicity, lifestyle, age and occupation group, for example.
- changes in the incidence of illnesses and deaths resulting from health promotion and improvement strategies such as immunization and health education programmes, for example.
- Variations in morbidity, mortality and health experience as a result of public health initiatives such as pollution control, sanitation or water quality projects, for example.

Epidemiological studies play a major part in public health planning and intervention. The data they provide influence health policy decisions at local and national levels, particularly through identifying risk factors for disease and illness and by enabling policy makers to set targets for health improvement and preventative health care provision.

See also – Clinical trial; Morbidity; Mortality.

Epithelial tissue

Epithelial tissues are continuous sheets of tissue that line the structures and cavities of the body. Different forms of epithelial tissue exist, including:

- Simple squamous epithelium consisting of one layer of cells. These can be found on the surface of lung alveoli where gases (oxygen and carbon dioxide) pass through them.
- Stratified squamous epithelium are layers of cells that can be replaced continuously. They are found in the skin and in places like the mouth, tongue, oesophagus and vagina.

Epithelial tissues act as barriers keeping different body systems separate. The ciliated epithelial tissue in the nose also forms a hair-like carpet that cleans air going into the respiratory tract by trapping dust and other particles and removing them in mucous.

See also – Cells; Gaseous exchange; Reproductive system; Tissue.

ABC GUIDE TO ANATOMY AND PHYSIOLOGY

Fluid balance

Fluid balance is an essential process – an aspect of homeostasis – within the human body. In basic terms, the amount of water in the human body must be controlled so that electrolyte (salts) levels in body fluids remain within healthy ranges. The amount of water taken into the body must equal (replace) the amount of water excreted from the body to maintain a healthy fluid balance.

Fluid is lost from the human body through respiration (breathing), perspiration (sweating), urination, defecation and expectoration (coughing, vomiting). Fluid intake is achieved through eating, drinking and parenteral means (e.g via an intravenous drip or gastrostomy / stomach feeding tube). The term 'evolemia' is used to describe the normal level body fluid volume. Hypovolemia (too little) and hypervolemia (too much) describe fluid imbalances within the body.

Fluid imbalance can occur during very hot weather through profuse sweating or through more extreme forms of exercise (e.g marathon running) or activity. In these cases electrolytes may be lost and the person may experience headaches, fatigue, vomiting and even death due to dehydration. Severe food poisoning, diarrhea and diabetes insipidus may also result in a person becoming dangerously dehydrated. Fluid, ideally containing salt or electrolytes, must be given in these circumstances. A person who consumes too much water, diluting the electrolyte salt levels in their body (hyponatremia), may also become very unwell with symptoms ranging from headaches, vomiting, and seizures to coma.

HEALTH AND SOCIAL CARE

Fluid balance is monitored closely in general hospital settings as it provides important information on an individual's state of hydration, renal and cardiovascular function. A person whose fluid loss is greater than their input has a negative fluid balance and will be given fluids (often intravenously) to compensate for this. A person with a positive fluid balance may, however, have a renal or cardiovascular problem.

See also – Homeostasis; Homeostatic failure

Foetal development

The growth and development of the baby in the uterus (womb) is one of the most eventful periods of human growth and development. It usually takes place over 37 to 42 weeks (full-term pregnancy) and can be divided into three different phases, known as trimesters.

The first trimester
The first twelve weeks of pregnancy are referred to as the first trimester. Once the fertilised ovum has implanted in the wall of the uterus, the embryo will begin to grow and develop. This is a critical time in the pregnancy. The growing embryo is nourished directly from the mother's blood through the placenta, to which it is attached by the umbilical cord. It receives both nutrients and oxygen in this way so does not breath normally or need to digest food. The embryo is protected in the uterus within the amniotic sac and surrounded by amniotic fluid. This protective environment keeps the embryo at a constant temperature and helps to prevent some infections.

From the eighth week of pregnancy, the embryo is referred to as a foetus. Most of the major body organs are formed during this period, although they will take more time to reach full maturity. By twelve weeks, an average foetus measures 6 cm (2.5 in) and weighs 9-14g (0.5 oz).

The second trimester

The second trimester of the pregnancy occurs between weeks 12 and 25. It is a period of rapid growth for the foetus and from about week 20 the pregnant woman can usually feel the foetus kicking. By 24 weeks, the foetus is considered to be viable, or able to survive on its own outside of the uterus. At this stage an average foetus measures 21 cm (8 in) and weighs 700 g (1.5 lb). Most women will appear to be noticeably pregnant during this trimester as the uterus increases in size and the breasts also enlarge.

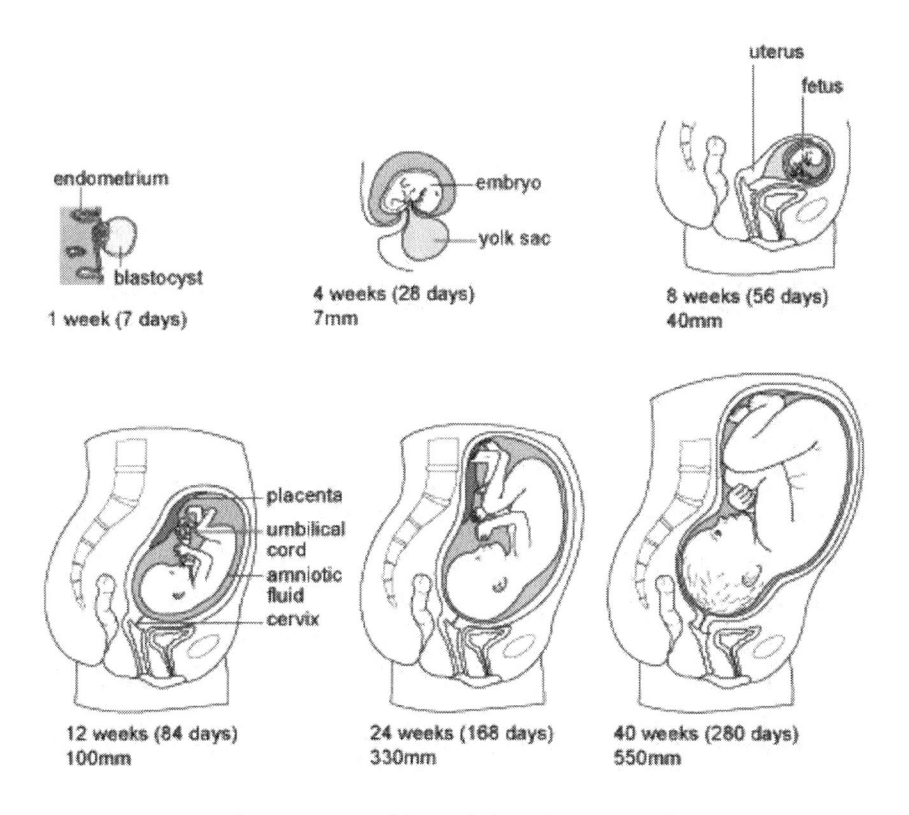

Figure 25 – An illustration of foetal development during pregnancy.

The third trimester

This is the period from week 25 until full term (between 37 and 42 weeks). The foetus will grow very rapidly during this time in preparation for birth and life outside of the uterus. Towards the end of the third trimester, the baby will settle low in the uterus with the head facing downwards (engaged). Occasionally, the baby will settle with its bottom, legs or feet facing downwards (breech position), but in most cases it will turn around before the birth. At full-term, an average baby measures 55cm (22in) and weighs 3.5k g (7lb 7oz). Many women experience tiredness and backache at this stage in the pregnancy as the foetus is quite heavy now.

See also – Amniocentesis; Chorionic villus sampling; Conception; Endometriosis; Reproductive system; Uterus

HEALTH AND SOCIAL CARE

Fractures

A fracture is a broken bone. Fractures can occur because of injury or disease.

There are six main types of fracture:

- Simple fractures (also known as closed fractures) occur where a bone breaks but does not damage the tissue around it.
- Compound fractures occur where a bone breaks and pierces the skin. They are also known as open fractures.
- Comminuted fractures occur where a bone breaks in several places.
- Impacted fractures involve a bone breaking and then one fractured end being shunted into the other.
- Greenstick fractures are incomplete fractures in long soft, flexible bones that are especially common in children.
- Complicated fractures are broken bones that also damage the tissues and sometimes the organs around them.

Types of Fractures

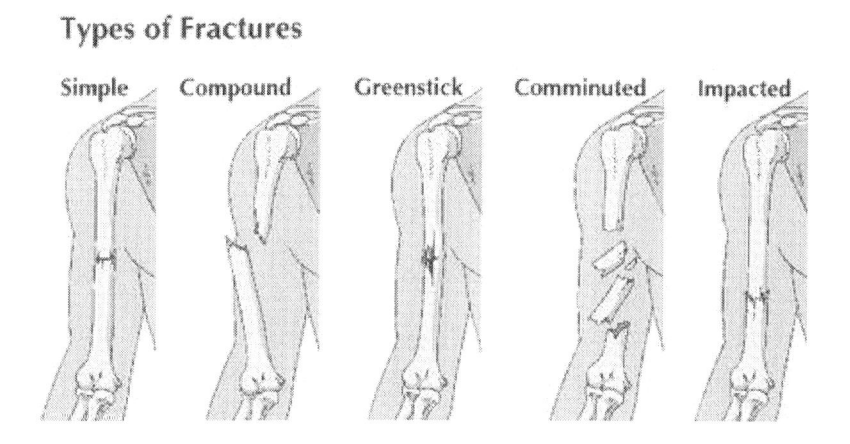

Figure 26 – Examples of fractures

See also – Bone; Skeletal system.

Gaseous exchange

The term gaseous exchange describes the movement of oxygen and carbon dioxide from the air in the lungs to the blood by diffusion.

At the surface of the alveoli, oxygen dissolves in the thin lining of moisture. The dissolved oxygen diffuses through the thin membrane into the blood. In the blood, haemoglobin reacts with the oxygen and locks it into the red blood cells to be carried around the body. Since the blood is always moving oxygenated blood is always being carried away from the alveoli. At the same time, unoxygenated red blood cells from the body are always arriving. This maintains a steep concentration gradient for oxygen to encourage rapid diffusion. The blood that arrives at the alveoli is rich in carbon dioxide. This diffuses out of the blood into the air in the lungs and can then be breathed out.

See also – Blood; Cardiovascular system; Chronic Obstructive Pulmonary Disease; Lungs; Pneumonia; Respiratory system.

HEALTH AND SOCIAL CARE

Heart

The heart is a muscular organ that plays a central, pumping role in the human circulatory system.

The heart's vital function is to pump blood to the lungs and around the body. Blood delivers oxygen, nutrients, hormones and antibodies to the areas of the body that need them. A normal size adult human heart is about the size of a clenched fist and is located in the thoracic cavity either side of the lungs. The heart and lungs are protected by the rib cage.

Structure of the heart

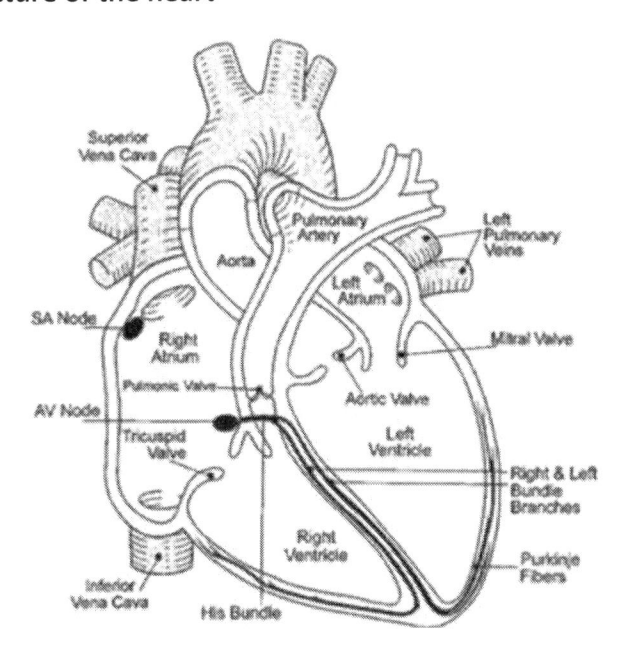

Figure 27 shows the structure of the heart.

The heart has four chambers joined together to make one large block of muscle. Specifically:

- the heart is structured around a muscular upper chamber called the atrium and a lower chamber called the ventricle
- because there are two sides to the heart, there are four heart chambers (a right and left atrium and a right and left ventricle)
- each chamber of the heart has a major blood vessel entering or leaving it
- the pulmonary artery leaves the right ventricle and takes blood to the lungs
- pulmonary veins return the blood (now carrying oxygen) to the heart via the left atrium
- the aorta is the main artery carrying blood to the body that exits the left ventricle
- the vena cava is the main vein bringing blood from the head and neck (superior vena cava) and the rest of the body (inferior vena cava) back to the heart
- there are valves between the atria and ventricles, known as atrioventricular valves, that ensure blood flows only one way though the heart
- the pulmonary artery and aorta also have valves, known as semi-lunar valves, to ensure that the blood which is pumped out of the heart doesn't re-enter the ventricles when the heart relaxes between beats.

In a resting adult human, the heart beats roughly 70 times per minute and will complete 2.5 million beats in an average lifetime.

Blood circulation through the heart

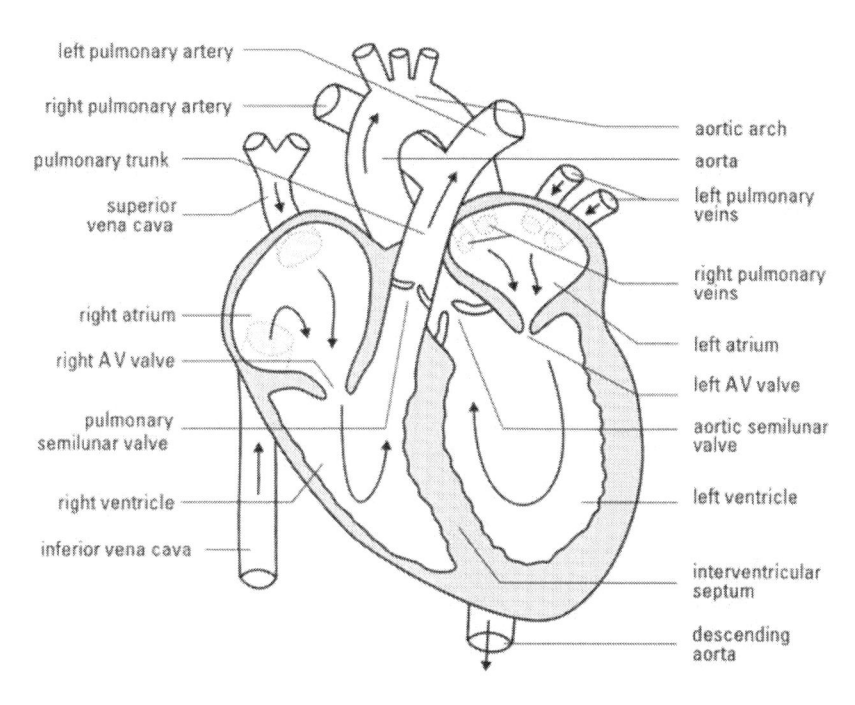

Figure 28 indicates the way blood flows through the heart.

Figure 28 illustrates how the right side of the heart (right atrium and ventricle) pumps blood to the lungs to pick up oxygen. The left side of the heart (left atrium, left ventricle) then pumps the oxygenated blood through the arteries to tissues around the body. Deoxygenated blood is then returned to the heart through the body's network of veins. Specifically:

- the pulmonary artery carries deoxygenated blood from the right ventricle to the lungs. It divides into two (the right and left pulmonary arteries) just outside the heart itself so that it can carry blood to both lungs.
- blood enters each atrium through pulmonary veins and leaves the heart through arteries in the ventricles
- the aorta is the main artery that takes blood from the left ventricle to the body

- the main vein bringing deoxygenated blood back to the heart from the body via the right atrium is the vena cava.

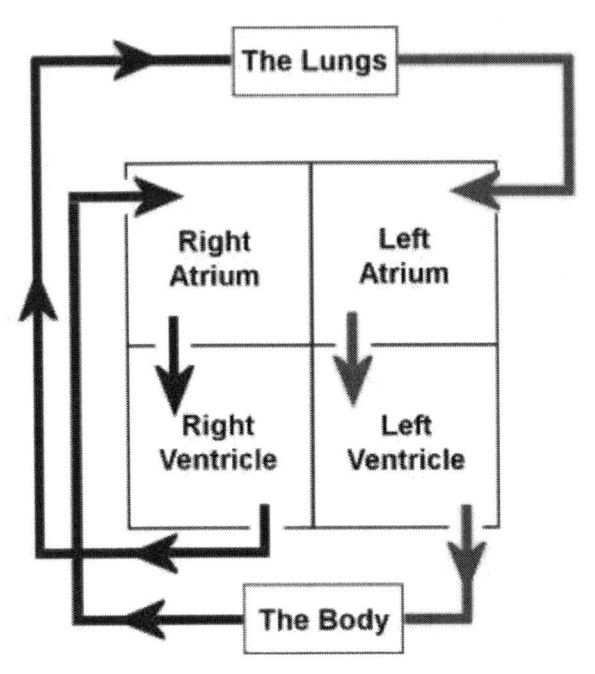

Figure 29 – An illustration of blood flow through the heart.

> ***See also*** – Blood; Blood pressure; Blood vessels; Coronary heart disease; Cardiovascular system; Hypertension; Pulmonary circulation; Stroke.

Hepatitis

Hepatitis is a general diagnostic terms that is used to describe pathological inflammation of the liver.

The main causes of hepatitis are viral infection and liver damage caused by excessive consumption of alcohol. There are a number of different types of hepatitis. Some have less serious health consequences than others which can become chronic, cause cirrhosis (scarring of the liver), loss of liver function or liver cancer.

The main symptoms of acute hepatitis include:

- fatigue
- muscle, joint and abdominal pain
- high temperature
- feeling nauseas and vomiting
- loss of appetite
- pale, grey-coloured faeces
- yellowing (jaundice) of the eyes and skin

Chronic hepatitis may have few symptoms until the person's liver starts to fail and may first be diagnosed through a blood test. In its advanced stages, the symptoms of chronic hepatitis include:

- jaundice
- swollen legs, ankles and feet
- blood in faeces and vomit
- confusion

There are a number of different forms of Hepatitis, including:

- Hepatitis A, caused by a virus that is usually contracted through ingesting food or fluids that contain traces of faeces. Healthcare staff and people travelling to areas where the virus is common

should be given a Hepatitis A vaccine. The symptoms of Hepatitis A generally last a few months but can be very uncomfortable.
- Hepatitis B is also caused by a virus but this is spread through the blood of an infected person. It is commonly spread through unprotected sex, injecting drug use and from pregnant women to their developing babies. Most people can fight off the Hepatitis B virus though it can become a chronic health problem and lead to cirrhosis and liver cancer if left untreated. Healthcare workers, gay men and people who inject drugs should obtain the Hepatitis B vaccine to reduce their higher risk of contracting it.
- Hepatitis C, caused by the Hepatitis C virus that is spread through blood-to-blood contact with an infected person. Typically, this form of hepatitis is contracted through sharing needles to inject drugs or through poor dental or healthcare practice (reusing unsterilised equipment). Many people are unaware they have the infection and only develop flu-like symptoms. About a quarter of people fight off the infection without treatment and remain virus free. The remaining people continue to carry the virus and are at risk of developing cirrhosis and liver failure. There is no vaccine for hepatitis C though anti-viral medication does provide very effective treatment.

See also – Liver

Hodgkin's disease

Hodgkin's disease, also known as Hodgkin lymphoma, is a rare form of cancer that develops and spreads through the lymphatic system. It is caused by a DNA mutation in B lymphocyte white blood cells. The cause of this mutation is currently unknown.

Cancer occurs when the 'instructions' contained in their DNA cause them to multiply uncontrollably rather than in a predictable, orderly way. In Hodgkin lymphoma, abnormal B lymphocytes start to multiply uncontrollably in one or more lymph nodes, and are felt or seen as a small, hard but painless lump or swelling particularly in the neck, armpit or groin. The abnormal lymphocytes may then spread to other parts of the body via the lymphatic system.

The precise reasons why a person develops Hodgkin lymphoma are currently unknown. Young adults in their early twenties, men rather than women and older adults over seventy years of age are most likely to develop this condition. A person's risk of developing the condition is higher if they:

- have a condition that weakens their immune system
- take medication that suppresses their immune system
- have had glandular fever (Epstein-Barr virus)
- have a biological relative (parent, sibling) who has had Hodgkin lymphoma.

Hodgkin lymphoma is not infectious. However, it is a relatively aggressive cancer that can spread quickly through the body. At the same time, it is relatively straightforward to treat with chemotherapy and radiotherapy. Most people who develop the condition will be successfully treated.

See also – Blood; Cells; Lymphatic system.

Homeostasis

The human body has the ability to regulate and maintain a stable internal (physiological) environment. This is known as homeostasis. This ability gives the body the ability to respond to changes in the external environment. For example, when the weather is very hot or very cold, homeostatic mechanisms in the body notice and make adjustments to the way the body functions. The temperature of the main organs in your body will not drop much below 36C or rise above 37C in either situation.

The liver, kidneys and brain are the main organs involved in homeostasis:

- the liver breaks down toxic substances and carbohydrates
- the kidneys regulate water levels, excrete waste products and clean the blood
- the hypothalamus in the brain is the control centre responding to changes that occur in the environment

Almost every aspect of your body's chemistry is controlled by a homeostatic mechanism to stop it drifting outside these limits. Homeostasis works through a negative feedback system. This means that when changes are noticed in the body's external environment, the body takes action to correct any deficits or deficiencies in order to maintain a constant internal environment.

The range of physiological processes in the body are controlled through homeostasis include heart rate, breathing rate, body temperature and blood glucose levels.

See also – Body temperature maintenance; Homeostatic failure; Negative feedback.

Homeostatic failure

Homeostasis does *not* mean that the body tries to keep everything constant. Homeostatic control mechanisms only start to work when a particular factor strays beyond the acceptable range. For example, blood sugar level is kept between 70 and 110 mg/100ml of blood. Anywhere within that range is 'safe' or 'normal'. It is only when the level rises above the upper threshold that the body reacts and tries to force it back down into the 'safe' range.

So, when looking at a factor like blood sugar, or temperature, remember that it will probably be controlled by a homeostatic mechanism and that it will have a 'normal' range. Some ranges are very narrow. For example, even a drop of 0.5 degrees centigrade in the temperature of the brain is very serious. A similar drop in the fingers would be quite safe and even normal on cold winter days when you have forgotten your gloves!

Figure 30 - A selection of normal values

Factor	Normal range
Blood sugar	70-110 mg/100ml
Blood pH	7.35-7.45
Body temperature	36.3-37.1 centigrade
O2 conc	>10.6 kPa
CO2 conc	4.7-6 kPa
Haemoglobin	Male: 13-18g/dL Female: 11.5-16g/dL
White cells (all types)	4-11 x 10^9/l
Cholesterol	4-<6mmol/l
Protein	60-80g/l
Urea levels	8-25mg/100ml
Heart rate at rest	70 bpm
Breathing rate at rest	12-15 breaths/min

See also – Autonomic nervous system; Body temperature maintenance; Diabetes; Homeostasis; Negative feedback

Huntington's chorea

Huntington's disease is a neurodegenerative disorder that is caused by a genetically transmitted gene mutation. The condition gradually impairs a person's muscle coordination, mental abilities and behavioural control.

The onset of Huntington's disease symptoms is subtle and often not noticed except by the person themselves and those very close to them. Early symptoms include mild mood or cognitive (memory, thinking, decision-making) problems. A more obvious unsteady gait and poor physical coordination follow. The characteristic symptoms of uncoordinated, jerky movements of the neck, arms and legs, physical rigidity and declining mental abilities gradually appear over a twenty-year period after the initial onset of symptoms.

Behavioural control problems related to apathy, irritability, anxiety and depressed mood are also often a feature of a person's declining ability to function independently. Both the physical and mental symptoms described result from the gradual failure of the person's brain to function normally. In particular, neurological changes prevent the brain from creating, sending and controlling 'signals' to other parts of the person's body. This is why a person's movement and mental state become difficult for them to control.

Frequent falls, increased risk of heart disease and pneumonia and the onset of dementia reduces the life expectancy of a person with Huntington's disease to approximately twenty years following the initial onset of their symptoms. People are typically aged between thirty-five and forty-four years of age when they first experience symptoms but may be younger or older than this in some cases.

HEALTH AND SOCIAL CARE

Many people are able to live independently for a long time if they receive assistance from family and friends or are able to obtain appropriate services. However, the very high levels of basic care and assistance required usually leads to people being supported in full-time residential care during the latter stages of their life.

Figure 31

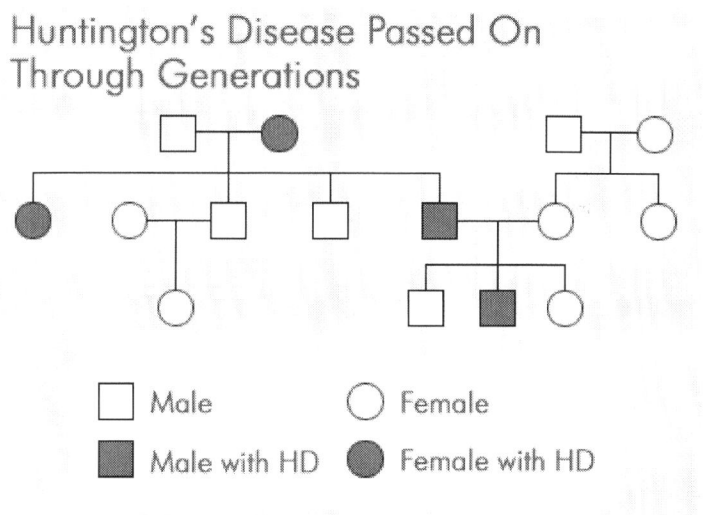

Huntington's Disease Passed On Through Generations

- ☐ Male
- ◯ Female
- ■ Male with HD
- ● Female with HD

See also – Brain; Central Nervous system; Mendelian Inheritance Principles; Muscular system.

ABC GUIDE TO ANATOMY AND PHYSIOLOGY

Hypertension

This is a medical term for high blood pressure. A person is considered to have high blood pressure (hypertension) when their blood pressure is consistently recorded as 180/110 mmHg or higher.

Blood pressure is measured in millimetres of mercury (mmHg) using an electronic or manual blood pressure monitor. The monitor takes two measurements and the person's blood pressure is then recorded as two figures, such as 140/80. The force, or pressure, which the blood puts on the walls of the artery when the heart beats and pushes the blood out into the circulatory system is the first of these measurements. This is known as the *systolic* blood pressure and is the larger or first number in the blood pressure reading. The continuous pressure that the person's blood puts on the arteries between heart beats is the second measurement and smaller number. Technically, this is known as the *diastolic* blood pressure. A healthy young adult will have a blood pressure reading of 120/80 mmHg (millimetres of mercury) or below but anything under 130/80 mmHg is considered normal.

In most cases people who have high blood pressure are unaware that they are hypertensive as there are no obvious, definitive symptoms. Some people with high blood pressure do get regular headaches, experience shortness of breath and get blurred vision because of it. However, most people only find out they are hypertensive when their blood pressure is measured by a healthcare or fitness professional

Where there is no specific, easily identifiable cause of a person's high blood pressure, a medical practitioner is likely to diagnose primary or essential hypertension. A number of factors increase a person's risk of developing primary hypertension including:

- Age – risk increases with age
- A family history of high blood pressure (genetics)
- Being of African or Caribbean origin (genetics)
- High salt intake
- Being overweight or obese
- Smoking
- Large alcohol intake

High blood pressure that is caused by another underlying medical or physical health problem is known as secondary hypertension. For example, people who have kidney disease, diabetes or Cushing's syndrome or who use recreational drugs such as cocaine or amphetamines may experience high blood pressure as a result of this.

Eating a balanced diet low in salt and fat but high in fibre, fruit and vegetables, staying within recommended intake levels for alcohol, reducing tea and coffee intake, avoiding smoking, maintaining a healthy weight and taking regular exercise are all effective ways to prevent or reduce high blood pressure. People who are unable to reduce their high blood pressure by making lifestyle changes may be prescribed one or more types of blood pressure-lowering medication by their GP.

See also – Blood pressure; Blood vessels; Cardiovascular system; Heart; Stroke.

Ileum

The Ileum is the final, and longest, part of the small intestine. It is about 3.5 metres (11.5 feet) long when stretched out. It extends from the middle section of the small intestine, the jejunum, to the colon (large intestine). The function of the ileum is to:

- digest vitamin B12, Folic acid and Vitamin C.
- absorb nutrients from food.

The walls of the ileum are lined with smooth muscle and are thinner and less permeable than the upper parts of the small intestine. Patches of lymphatic tissue (known as Peyer patches) as well as receptors for bile salts and vitamin B12 are embedded in the wall of the ileum aiding the absorption of nutrients.

See also - Alimentary canal; Digestive system; Digestion; Muscle; Lymphatic system.

Intestines

The intestines are part of the alimentary canal, extending from the stomach to the anus. The human intestine consists of two segments, the large and small intestine.

The small intestine is a greyish purple colour, 35 millimetres in diameter and about 6-7 meters (20-23 feet) long in an average adult. It is divided into three parts; the duodenum, the jejunum and the ileum. The walls of the small intestine consist of a muscular layer, a layer containing blood vessels, lymph vessels and nerves and an inner mucous membrane layer. This inner layer is covered with villi which increase the surface area for absorption and also contain a network of lymph and blood vessels. The main function of the small intestine is to break down, digest and absorb nutrients from food.

The large intestine is dark red in colour and about 1.5 meters long. It sits in the same abdominal space and is draped around the small intestine. The large intestine consists of the caecum, appendix, colon, rectum, anal canal and anus. Its function is to reabsorb water and nutrients from digestive waste and then to get rid of waste. It does this by storing undigested food as faeces until it is passed out of the body through the anus.

See also – Alimentary canal; Digestion; Digestive system; Ileum.

Joints

Joints are the skeleton's hinges that enable different parts of the body to move.

The three main types of joint in the human body are:

- Synovial or freely moveable joints (see below for examples)
- Cartilaginous or slightly moveable joints (e.g spine)
- Fibrous or fixed joints (e.g skull)

There are a number of different sub-types of synovial joint including:

- Ball and socket joints (e.g hip and shoulder joints) that allow a broad range of movement
- Gliding joints (e.g tarsals and carpals in the hands) that glide over each other but have very limited movement otherwise
- Hinge joints (e.g elbow, knee, ankle) that move in one direction only
- Saddle joints (e.g wrist and thumb) that move around two axes allowing a limited range of movement

Cartilaginous joints move through the compression of cartilage. Fibrous joints on, the other hand, don't move at all.

See also – Bone; Skeletal system.

Kidneys

The kidneys are bean-shaped organs about 11cm long that weigh between 115 and 170g in adults. Humans have two kidneys, located behind the abdominal cavity, one on each side of the spine just below the level of the diaphragm. The left kidney is usually slightly larger than the right.

Diagram of Kidney

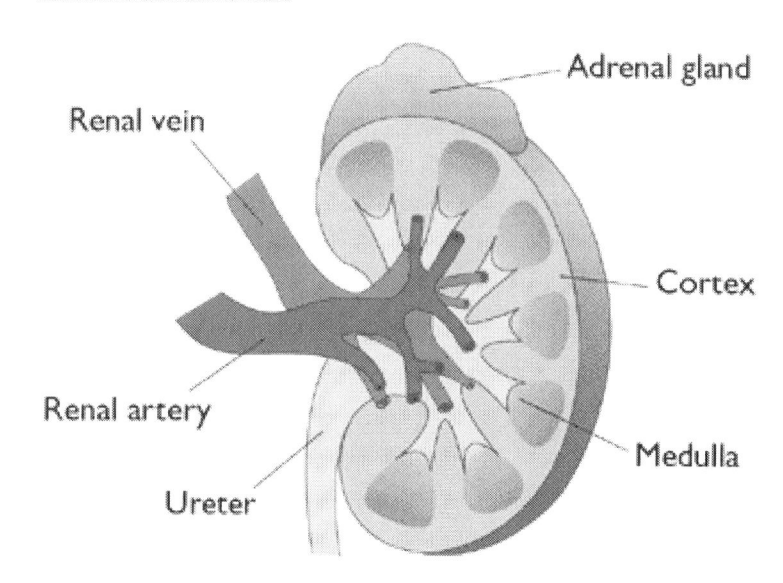

Figure 32 – The internal structure of a kidney

ABC GUIDE TO ANATOMY AND PHYSIOLOGY

The kidney has a two-part structure: the medulla on the inside and the cortex on the outside. The medulla leads to the renal pelvis, a cavity that connects the medulla to the ureter. Blood vessels, lymphatic vessels, nerves and the ureter enter the centre of the kidney and are located in the hilum. Kidney tissue consists of twisted tubes called nephrons that filter blood and excrete waste products.

The kidneys carry out a number of functions for the body including:
- filtering out and removing excess salt, water and waste products from the blood before recirculating it.
- reabsorbing useful materials needed by the body.
- keeping the composition of their blood balanced by maintaining correct levels of minerals, salts and fluids.
- producing urine.

See also – Renal system; Urinary tract infection

Leukaemia

Leukaemia is a form of blood cell cancer.

There are a number of types of leukaemia including:
- acute myeloid leukaemia
- acute lymphoblastic leukaemia
- chronic myeloid leukaemia
- chronic lymphocytic leukaemia

Acute leukaemia is an aggressive form of the disease that occurs when stem cells in the bone marrow produce too many immature white blood cells. These so-called 'blast cells' can't fight infection effectively and also cause a drop in oxygen-carrying red blood cell and platelet production. The two main types of white blood cells affected by acute leukaemia are:

- lymphocytes – mostly used to fight viral infections
- myeloid cells – which fight bacterial infections, defend the body against parasites and prevent the spread of tissue damage

A person with acute myeloid leukaemia is likely to be become increasingly unwell over a couple of weeks and needs immediate treatment. Their symptoms may include:

- pale skin
- breathlessness
- tiredness
- frequent infections
- bleeding gum or nosebleeds

The cause of acute myeloid leukaemia is a DNA mutation in the stem cells of a person's bone marrow. What triggers this mutation is unclear. Factors such as previous chemo- or radiotherapy, exposure to high levels of radiation, the chemical benzene or having

ABC GUIDE TO ANATOMY AND PHYSIOLOGY

an underlying blood or genetic disorder (e.g Down's syndrome) are associated with a higher risk of developing the condition. Leukaemia is diagnosed by blood tests that assess blood cell production. Because leukaemia is a rapidly developing condition, treatment should start as soon as possible after diagnosis.

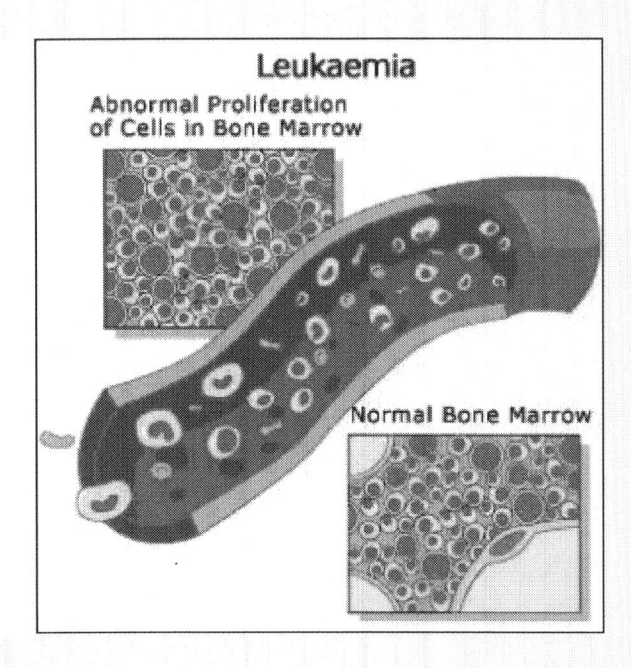

Figure 33 – Acute leukaemia is the result of a DNA mutation in bone marrow stem cells.

See also – Cells; Blood

Liver

The liver is the largest internal organ in the human body. It is on the right side of the abdominal cavity just below the diaphragm.

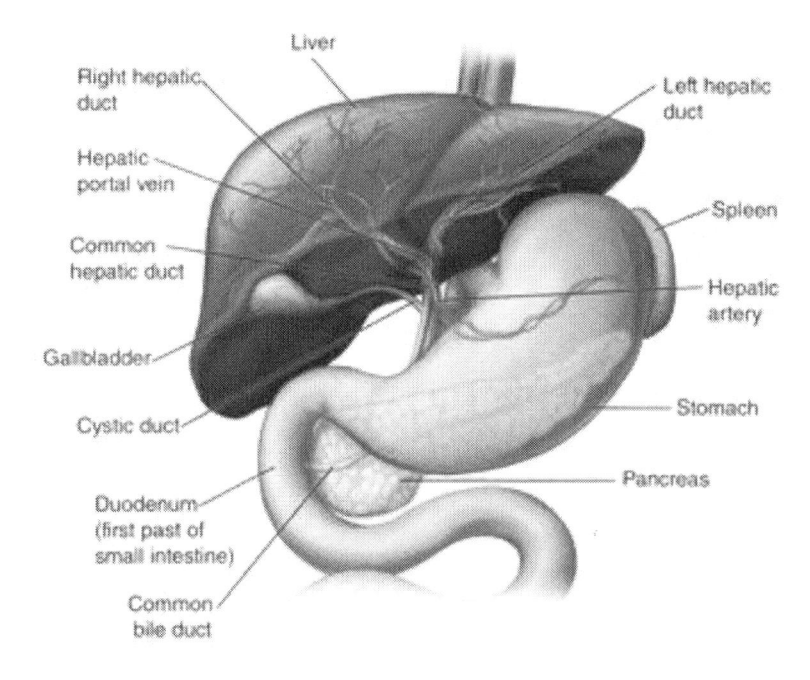

Figure 34 – An illustrated cross-section of the liver.

The liver performs a number of essential functions for the human body including:

- storing iron and some vitamins (A, B12, D, E, K)
- removing toxins (e.g drugs and alcohol) from the blood
- helping to control levels of glucose in the blood
- producing heat that keeps the body warm
- producing Vitamin A and Vitamin D
- producing bile salts that break down fat in the small intestines
- converting stored fats into other fat products (e.g cholesterol) and stored glycogen to glucose when energy is needed

See also – Hepatitis.

Lungs

The lungs are two spongy organs located in the chest (thorax) on either side of the heart that are central to human respiration (breathing).

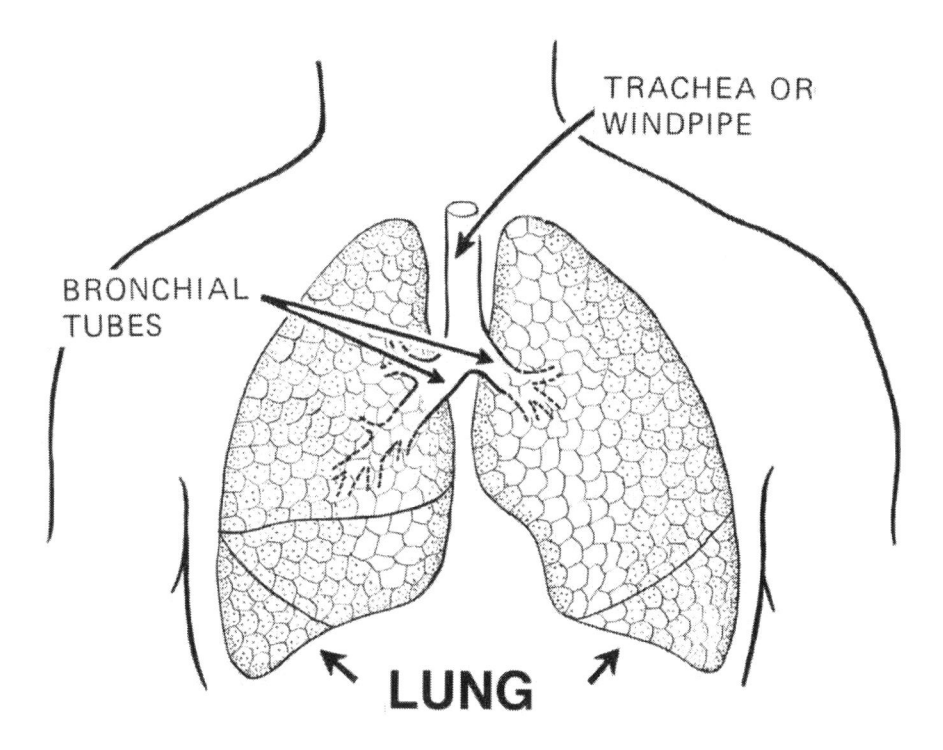

Figure 35 – An illustration of lungs and the airways that support human respiration.

The two main functions of the lungs are to:

- transport oxygen from the atmosphere into the bloodstream
- remove carbon dioxide from the bloodstream and release it into the atmosphere.

A typical pair of human lungs weighs just over a kilogram and fit into a space that measures less than 40 cm from top to bottom. However, they contain over 80m^2 of surface area for gaseous exchange. The skin surface area in the same person is roughly two square metres. The enormous surface area in the lungs depends on 500 million small sacs called alveoli. Alveoli (singular alveolus) are balloon-like swellings on the ends of bronchioles. They are made of a thin membrane covered with tiny blood vessels.

The bronchioles are the thinnest tubes in the lungs. They carry air directly into the alveoli. Bronchioles connect to the bronchi rather like the branches on a tree. The bronchi join together to form the trachea, also called the windpipe. Rings of stiff cartilage help to keep the trachea and bronchi from being squashed flat by the breathing movements. The ribs and sternum protect the lungs and heart.

See also – Cystic fibrosis; Gaseous exchange; Chronic Obstructive Pulmonary Disease (COPD); Pneumonia; Pulmonary circulation; Respiratory system.

Lymphatic system

The lymphatic system is part of the human body's immune system. It consists of a network of lymph vessels, lymphatic tissue and clumps of bean-shaped lymph glands or 'nodes'.

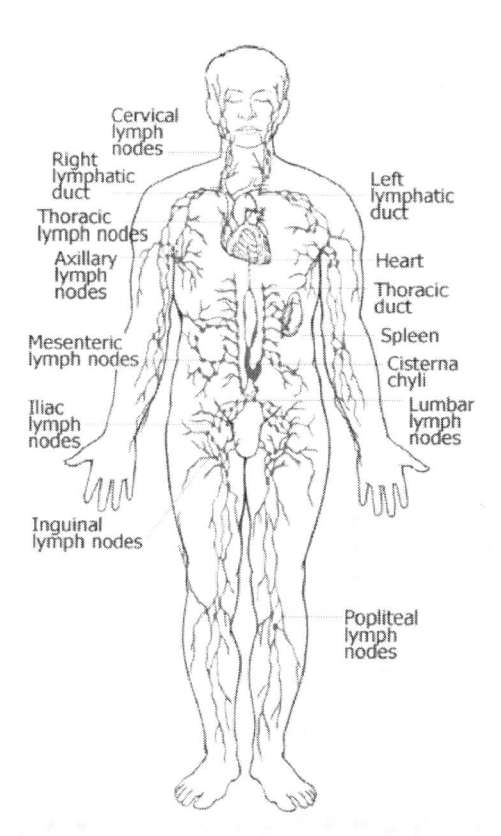

Figure 36 – The lymphatic system covers the whole of the human body.

Lymph vessels collect lymph fluid from body tissues and return it to the blood, helping to maintain fluid balance in the body. Clear lymph fluid contains electrolytes, proteins and infection-fighting white blood cells (lymphocytes). The lymphocytes have been produced in the bone marrow, spleen and thymus. Lymph fluid is collected from all over the body and passes through at least one of the almost 600 lymph nodes in the body. The lymph node is like a filtration system, destroying damaged cells, unwanted protein and bacteria. As part of this process, the lymphocyctes produce antibodies to boost the body's immune response to infection. Once the lymph fluid has been cleaned it enters the blood stream.

As well as the lymph system, a number of other components are involved in the complete lymphatic system. These include the thymus, red bone marrow found in flat bones and epiphyses of long bones in adults, the spleen and lymphatic nodules (tonsils and peyer's patch). The lymphatic system is essential for human health. Without it, body tissue would quickly swell up with fluid and waste products and would have little defence against infections that could rapidly overwhelm the body's essential organs.

See also – Blood; Endocrine system; Fluid balance; Hodgkin's disease.

HEALTH AND SOCIAL CARE

Mendelian inheritance principles

Gregor Mendel (1822 – 1884), a 19th century priest and scientist, is seen as the originator of the modern science of genetics. He established many of the rules or principles of heredity through carrying out experiments on pea plants.

Mendel's big discovery was that biological traits are handed down from parents to their offspring through what he called 'units of inheritance' (now known as 'genes'). In addition to this insight, Mendel also identified a number of principles that affect the way genetic inheritance works. The so-called 'dominance principle' is particularly important. This describes how a person inherits two genes (one from their father, one from their mother) for each biological trait (e.g eye colour, height etc). However, only one of these genes can be expressed. Mendel worked out that the genes we inherit are either dominant or recessive. The trait that is expressed always comes from the dominant gene, unless we inherit two recessive genes.

Modern genetic science has developed beyond studying basic gene function and behaviour but does still include this as a significant focus. The structure, function and distribution of genes and their influence on various diseases, developmental processes and human behaviour is now a major part of modern genetics.

See also – Cells; Cell structure; Cystic fibrosis; Muscular dystrophy;

Morbidity

This term is used within medicine and epidemiology to refer to the incidence and distribution of diseases and illnesses within a population, social group or geographical location.

Public health statistics are often collated and produced to describe morbidity in relation to gender, social class, lifestyle, diet and patterns of consumption, occupational group, ethnicity and age. Public health specialists and academic social scientists also produce data that maps changes in morbidity over time in society.

Terms such as co-morbidity and multi-morbidity are sometimes used to describe patterns and situations where more than one disease, illness or condition is experienced simultaneously within a population or social group – such as depression and substance misuse, for example.

See also – Mortality; Epidemiological study

Mortality

The term mortality is used with healthcare practice and epidemiology to refer to death.

The mortality rate is an important statistic in epidemiological studies and public health work. It refers to the number of deaths in a given area or over a particular period of time, from a particular cause. Mortality statistics are often presented in age-bands so that death rates, and the likelihood of premature death, can be identified in a specific population of people.

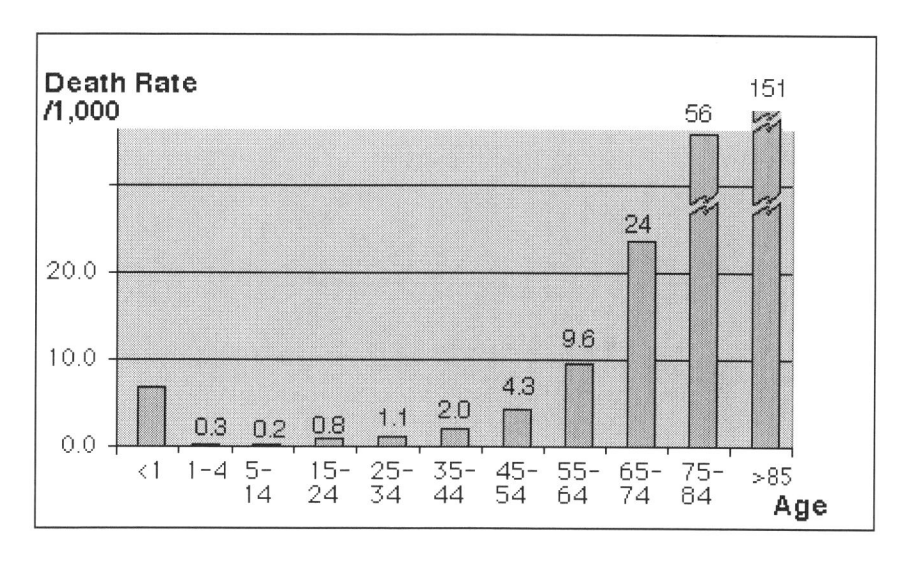

Figure 37 – An example of mortality statistics

See also – Morbidity; Epidemiological study

Multiple Sclerosis

Multiple sclerosis is an autoimmune condition in which a person's immune system attacks the myelin sheath that protects the nerves in the brain and/or spinal cord. It is classified as a neurological condition and usually diagnosed and treated by neurologists.

A person with multiple sclerosis experiences autoimmune attacks that cause the myelin sheath in their central nervous system to become inflamed in small patches. This disrupts the flow of electrical signals from the brain to various parts of the body. Scarring of the myelin sheath (sclerosis) is typically left behind when the inflammation dies down or goes away. However, frequent and repeated autoimmune attacks eventually lead to permanent nerve damage and disability.

A person with multiple sclerosis may experience some or all of the following symptoms:

- fatigue and loss of strength
- numbness or tingling in their limbs
- muscle stiffness and spasms
- difficulty walking, balancing and coordinating arm and leg movement
- vision problems, such as blurred vision
- bladder control problems
- problems with thinking, learning and planning

The cause(s) of multiple sclerosis, and the reasons why some people get it rather than others, is currently unknown. Scientists and neurologists with experience of researching, diagnosing and treating the condition believe that the causes are likely to be both genetic and environmental. Specifically, it is likely that people who develop MS have a genetic predisposition to it that is then triggered by external or environmental factors. Epidemiological studies have identified that rates of MS are higher in countries that lack sunlight and where people have low vitamin D levels, for example. Similarly, people who smoke are twice as likely to develop MS as people who don't. Infections, such as the Epstein-Barr virus, are also thought to trigger the kind of immune response that leads to MS.

There is currently no cure for multiple sclerosis. A person's symptoms may be partially relieved, and their progression slowed down, by medication, the use of complementary therapies and through the provision of occupational therapy and other forms of social care and support. A great deal depends on the severity and frequency of an individual's symptoms. Multiple sclerosis can have mild to very serious, life-limiting effects on those who develop this condition. It is more commonly diagnosed in women than men, with most people being diagnosed in their 20s and 30s. A person's symptoms may be intermittent, with them having periods of remission and then relapse, or it may be progressive and more disabling over time.

See also – Brain; Central nervous system.

Muscular dystrophy

Muscular dystrophy is a group of inherited, genetic disorders rather than a single, specific condition that cause progressive and increasingly disabling muscle weakness.

The cause of each type of muscular dystrophy is a gene mutation that affects the structure and functioning of the person's muscles. The gene mutation causes changes in the person's muscle fibres which then impairs the muscles' ability to function correctly. Some types of muscular dystrophy affect the heart (a muscle) or the respiratory muscles making them life-threatening conditions. However, other types of muscular dystrophy have relatively mild symptoms and don't affect life expectancy at all.

Duchenne muscular dystrophy is one of the most common, and most severe forms of muscular dystrophy. It typically affects boys in early childhood. Approximately 100 boys are born with Duchenne muscular dystrophy each year in the UK. There are about 2500 boys living with this condition at any one time. Because Duchenne muscular dystrophy is a progressive, life-limiting condition few survive beyond their 20s or early 30s.

Duchenne muscular dystrophy is present from birth but the symptoms may not be noticed for a few more years. Muscle weakness becomes more evident when a child tries to move independently and struggles to stand up, walk or climb stairs, for example. A GP will need to observe and examine a child, carry out blood tests and refer the child for specialist electrical tests on their muscles in addition to obtaining a muscle biopsy before a diagnosis can be made.

There is currently no cure for Duchenne muscular dystrophy. A number of treatments and forms of support are offered to children and young people living with this condition. These include:
- medication to improve muscle strength and treat heart disorders
- exercise, physiotherapy and mobility aids to assist with basic mobility
- support groups to provide social and emotional support
- surgery to correct postural deformities – particularly scoliosis.

The purpose of these treatments and interventions is to manage an individual's symptoms so they can live as well as possible with the condition they have.

See also – Mendelian Inheritance Principles; Muscle; Muscular system;

Muscular system

The muscular system consists of a range of specialised muscle tissues that enable the body to move whilst also giving it stability. Each type of muscle tissue performs a specific function within the human body. The muscular system is very closely linked, in many cases literally linked by tendons, to the skeletal system but also plays an important part in both the respiratory and cardiovascular systems.

The types of muscles that comprise the muscular system include:

- Skeletal muscles and their associated tissues. These are the visible muscles (in the bicep, for example) that people think of when the term 'muscle' is used. Skeletal muscles consist of coarse tissue that is designed to contact and move body parts. A person generally has conscious control of their skeletal muscles.
- Smooth muscle tissue. These can be found in the stomach, intestines and urinary system. They exert sub-conscious control over various body systems, controlling blood flow in major organs and regulating blood pressure, for example.

Tendons and ligaments are two other important features of the muscular system:

- A tendon connects a muscle to the bone that it will move. As a result, tendons must be both strong and flexible so that they can resist pressures that might tear or break them. Tendon strains and injuries (as well as tears and breakages) do still occur if they are over-extended or suffer a traumatic impact.
- A ligament connects two bones that are moved by skeletal muscles. They consist of fibrous material and are essential for providing skeletal stability during both movement and rest.

Adipose tissue is the final anatomical feature of the muscular system. This is a type of connective tissue that stores energy and insulates the body whilst also providing cushioning for joints. It is particularly important during sports and strenuous activity when skeletal-muscle contacts put joints under strain.

The functions of the muscular system include:

- *Movement of body parts* – skeletal muscles enable voluntary movement of human body parts through contraction. They do the mechanical work of the body, using energy from food to do so.
- *Stability and posture* – muscles give the human skeleton stability and the body proper posture. Many joints require the support of muscles to maintain stability.
- *Heat production* – the muscular system uses a large proportion of the energy produced by the body. As a result, muscles produce the greatest amount of heat in the body and are important for keeping the body warm.
- *Facilitating circulation* – cardiac muscles are vital for pumping blood throughout the human body. The muscular heart keeps blood moving, taking oxygen and nutrients to all tissues and removing waste products and carbon dioxide from the body.
- *Promoting digestion* – the smooth muscles of the digestive system play an essential part in the digestive process that creates energy and brings nutrients into the body.

See also – Bone; Muscle; Muscular dystrophy; Skeletal system;

Muscle

Muscle consists of fibrous tissue that produces movement in the body when it contracts. Muscles also protect the abdomen from injury and help to support the body.

Muscle tissues are unusual because they can contract and relax. They contain protein fibres, actin and myosin that cause movement when they slide over each other. There are three main types of muscular tissue (see figure 34).

Figure 38 – Main types of muscular tissue

Tissue type	Function
Skeletal (striated)	Attached to the skeleton, produces movement and maintains posture, can contract and relax rapidly and is under voluntary control.
Smooth (non-striated)	Found in tubular organs, glands, bronchioles, the reproductive system and the gut. This muscle tissue controls the movement of substances along the tubes. It is not under voluntary control and moves slowly.
Cardiac	Found in the heart. This has self-generating (myogenic) contractions that occur rapidly.

See also – Muscular dystrophy; Muscular system; Heart; Respiratory system; Skeletal system.

Negative feedback

Negative feedback is a process that responds to changes within human body systems to ensure they are kept within acceptable limits.

In negative feedback, a system will respond to any change by doing something that *reduces* the effect of the change on the system. For example, when you start to feel cold your body shivers. Shivering generates heat that warms the body up. If you drink a lot of water your body responds by making lots of dilute urine which passes out of the body and so reduces water content. If you hold your breath the carbon dioxide level in your blood rises. Your brain responds by forcing you to breathe more quickly as soon as you stop –so reducing the carbon dioxide level again. Even if you pass out when you hold your breath (and this is fortunately very difficult to do!) your brain takes over and forces you to breathe as soon as you lose consciousness.

Systems that show negative feedback tend to be stable and settle into a predictable pattern. In fact, most biological systems show negative feedback as it keeps them safely within healthy limits.

See also – Blood; Body temperature maintenance; Homeostasis; Homeostatic failure; Fluid balance.

Nervous tissue

Nervous tissue is composed of neurons (nerve cells) and neuroglial cells. The grey matter and white matter found in the central nervous system (brain and spinal cord) are examples of nervous tissue.

The function of nervous tissue is to control and co-ordinate the activities of the body. Receptor cells in the sense organs (eyes, ears, nose, mouth, skin) detect changes in the external and internal environment and send impulses along sensory neurones to the central nervous system (brain and spinal cord). The brain then processes this information and decides how to respond. Impulses are then sent along motor neurones to the muscles and glands in the body.

In effect, nervous tissue provides a communication network for the nervous system, sending electrical impulses across the tissue.

See also – Brain; Tissue; Central Nervous System;

Organs

An organ is a separate, recognisable body part, such as the liver or heart for example.

Organs are made up of more than one type of tissue. The different types of tissue within an organ have been grouped together in order to perform one or more specific functions in the human body.

Each of the various body organs carry out vital functions necessary to sustain life. These include absorbing food, pumping blood or producing a hormone. The lungs, liver, kidneys, stomach, intestines, brain and heart are the main organs present in both the male and female human body.

You need to know where the organs are located in the body and also how they work together as body systems.

ABC GUIDE TO ANATOMY AND PHYSIOLOGY

Organs

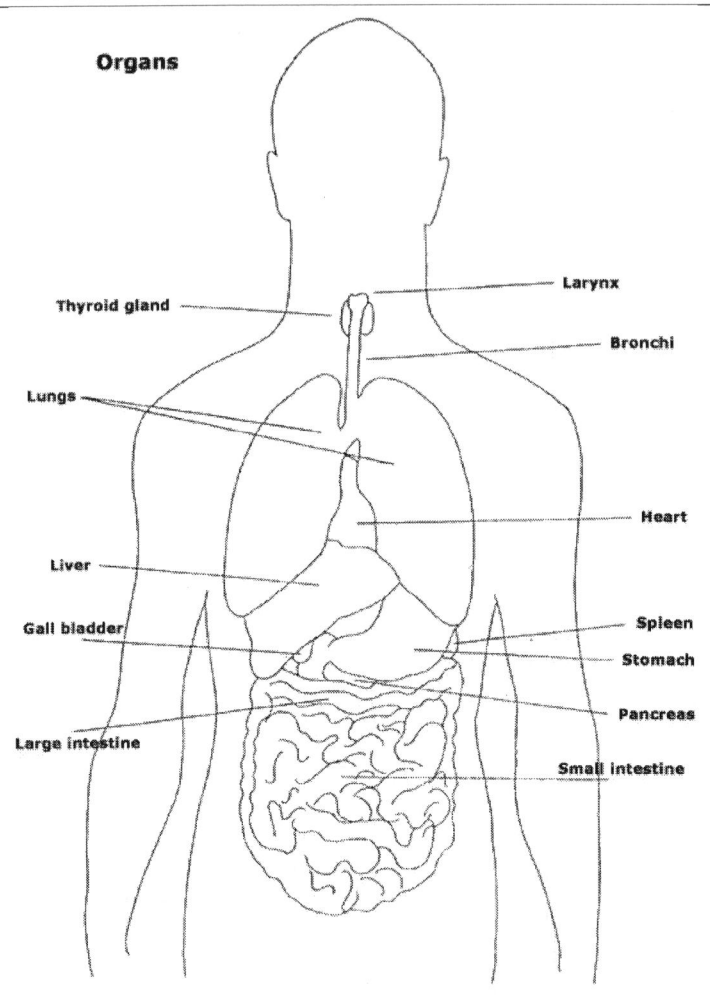

- Larynx
- Thyroid gland
- Bronchi
- Lungs
- Heart
- Liver
- Spleen
- Gall bladder
- Stomach
- Pancreas
- Large intestine
- Small intestine

Figure 39 – The location of organs in the human body

See also – Brain; Cardiovascular system; Cells; Digestive system; Endocrine system; Heart; Ileum; Intestines; Kidneys; Lungs; Pancreas; Renal system; Respiratory system; Stomach; Tissue;

Osteoarthritis

Osteoarthritis is a joint condition that results in tenderness, stiffness and pain. Joints affected by osteoarthritis are characterized by damage to, or loss of, the cartilage that protect them and allow them to move smoothly, the development of bony growths and inflammation around the joint. Virtually all joints can be affected by osteoarthritis but it is most likely to affect a person's knees, hips and the joints in their hands.

NORMAL JOINT   JOINT WITH OSTEOARTHRITIS

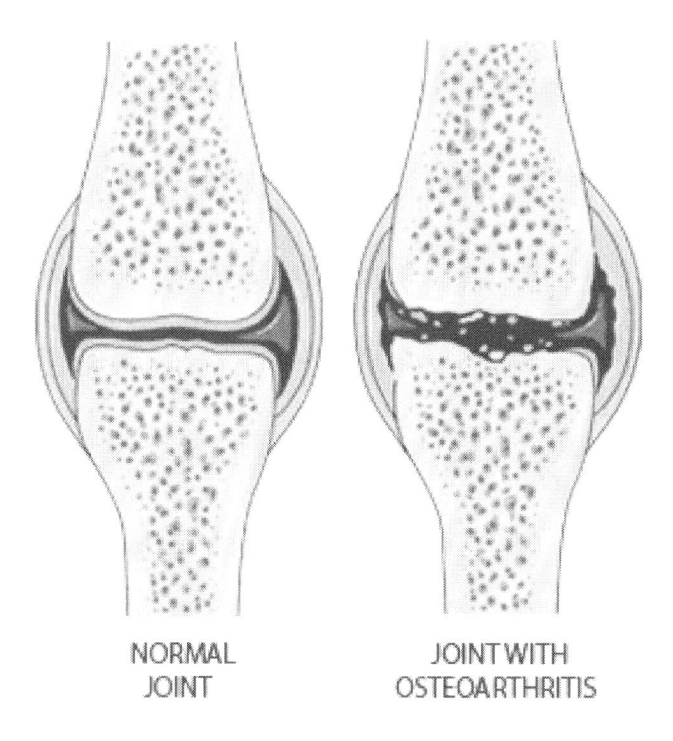

Figure 40 – An illustration of a normal knee joint and a knee joint affected by osteoarthritis.

People with osteoarthritis tend to notice the stiffness and experience pain in their joints when they haven't moved for a while. Getting up, moving around and trying to pick up or hold objects can be difficult. A person with osteoarthritis may also notice a grating feeling or crackling sound in their arthritic joints when they use them. Depending on the severity of a person's condition, they may experience a limited range of movement in their joints and experience weakness and muscle wasting in the affected areas of the body. The effects of osteoarthritis can sometimes be seen where a person's joints appear slightly larger or more 'knobbly' and lumpy than normal.

The symptoms of osteoarthritis can be mild and intermittent for some people but severe and continuous for others. Some people link their symptoms to their activity levels (especially lack of activity / exercise) whilst others believe that cold, damp weather triggers their symptoms.

There is no cure for osteoarthritis though it isn't necessarily progressive or degenerative either. People who are diagnosed with osteoarthritis may be prescribed medication, including painkillers and steroids, to help them cope with their symptoms. In many cases lifestyle changes such as doing regular exercise, losing weight and being active are also recommended.

See also – Bone; Joints; Skeletal system.

Osteoporosis

Osteoporosis is a relatively common bone condition that weakens a person's bones and makes them more likely to fracture.

Osteoporosis is diagnosed through a specialist bone density scan (a DEXA scan) that measures bone mineral density. A GP or hospital specialist is also likely to take a full personal health and family medical history to try to identify risk factors that may predispose a person to osteoporosis.

In addition to ageing, risk factors associated with osteoporosis include having:

- a co-existing inflammatory condition (such as rheumatoid arthritis), chronic obstructive pulmonary disorder (COPD) or Crohn's disease
- a condition that affects hormone production, such as an over- or under-active thyroid.
- a family history of osteoporosis.
- a body mass index (BMI) of 19 or less.

Long-term use of some medications that affect bone strength or hormone levels, heavy drinking or smoking also increase a person's risk of developing osteoporosis.

Many older people receive hospital treatment each year for fractures that are the result of osteoporosis. The most common fracture sites linked to osteoporosis are the wrist, hip and spinal vertebrae. A person with osteoporosis also has a higher risk of fracturing bones in their arm, their ribs or their pelvis. Fractures can occur as a result of even minor falls as a person with osteoporosis is often unaware that they have developed this condition.

People who are at higher risk of osteoporosis may be prescribed medication to strengthen their bones. Other forms of treatment focus on prevention of falls and avoidance of situations where this might happen. Regular exercise, eating a healthy diet (particularly foods rich in Vitamin D and calcium), as well as avoiding alcohol and not smoking, can all help to reduce risk too.

See also – Bones; Chronic Obstructive Pulmonary Disease; Fractures; Skeletal system

Pancreas

The pancreas is a gland located in the abdomen, behind the stomach and between the duodenum and spleen.

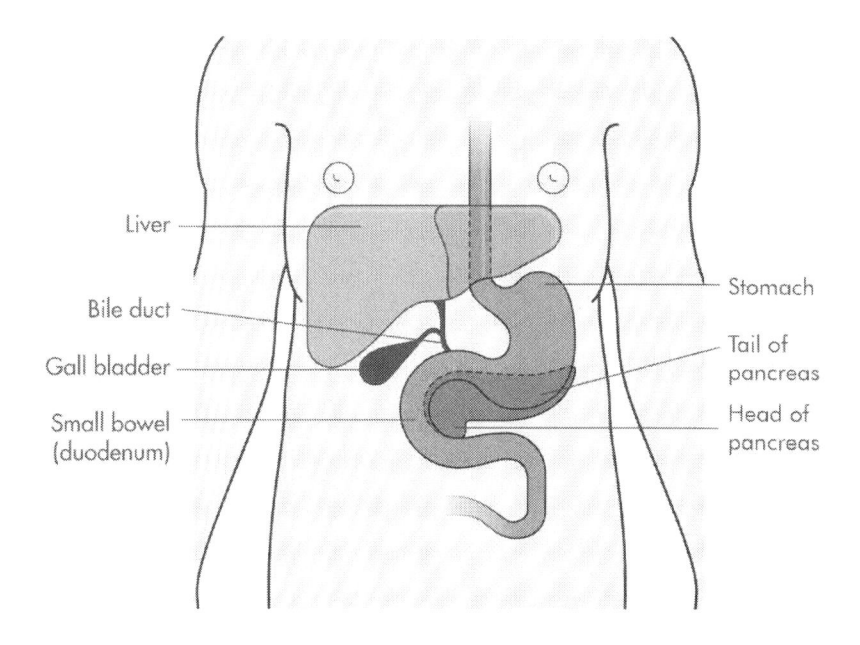

Figure 41 – The location of the pancreas

The function of the pancreas is to produce hormones (insulin) that control glucose levels in the blood after eating and to secrete enzymes (pancreatic juices) into the duodenum through the pancreatic duct that enable the body to break down and digest food. This means that the pancreas is both an essential part of the digestive system but also a part of the endocrine system.

See also – Diabetes; Digestion; Digestive system; Endocrine system.

ABC GUIDE TO ANATOMY AND PHYSIOLOGY

Parkinson's disease

Parkinson's disease is a neurological condition affecting the ability of the brain to function effectively. It is caused by the gradual loss of nerve cells in part of the brain called the *substantia nigra*. The loss of these nerve cells results in a reduction of dopamine in the brain and leads to the following symptoms of Parkinson's disease:

- involuntary tremors of particular parts of the body (hands, limbs especially)
- slow movement
- stiff, inflexible muscles

Dopamine is a naturally occurring chemical that acts as a neurotransmitter. It plays a critical role in enabling the brain to control movement. It is this shortage of dopamine, especially the death of dopamine neurons, that is thought to be responsible for those with Parkinson's disease being unable to execute smooth, controlled movements. The precise reasons for the loss of nerve cells is unknown. Medical scientists believe that a combination of genetic and environmental factors (pesticides, herbicides and industrial pollution) are responsible.

In addition to the movement-related symptoms of Parkinson's disease, people with this condition may also experience a range of other physical and psychological symptoms, including:

- depression and anxiety
- anosmis (loss of sense of smell)
- insomnia (difficulties sleeping)
- memory / recall problems

HEALTH AND SOCIAL CARE

There is currently no cure for Parkinson's disease. Treatments aim to minimize symptoms and help the person to manage their everyday living needs. Physiotherapy, occupational therapy and medication are the main forms of treatment most people with Parkinson's disease receive.

See also – Brain; Central Nervous System.

ABC GUIDE TO ANATOMY AND PHYSIOLOGY

Pneumonia

Pneumonia is a serious lung condition. It occurs when the lung becomes inflamed, usually because of a bacterial infection, and the alveoli fill up with fluid.

Pneumonia may have an acute (sudden) onset over a day or two or may develop more slowly over several days. The symptoms of pneumonia can include:

- a cough that may be dry or which produces thick, sometimes blood-flecked, phlegm or even blood itself (haemoptysis)
- shortness of breath, even when resting
- chest pain, especially when coughing
- headaches, joint and muscle pain
- loss of appetite, nausea and vomiting
- fast pulse / heartbeat
- raised temperature
- sweating and shivering
- feeling very tired, confused or disorientated

Pneumonia can affect people throughout the lifespan. However, babies and young children, older people, people with other serious health conditions and those with weakened immune systems are at greater risk of developing the condition.

See also – Respiratory system; Lungs; Pulmonary circulation

Pulmonary circulation

Because the blood passes through both sides of the heart in one cycle, the heart is said to have a double circulation. You may also come across the terms pulmonary circulation and systemic circulation.

Pulmonary circulation refers to the circulation of blood to and from the lungs. Specifically:

- the pulmonary artery carries deoxygenated blood from the right ventricle to the lungs. It divides into two (the right and left pulmonary arteries) just outside the heart itself so that it can carry blood to both lungs.
- blood enters each atrium through pulmonary veins and leaves the heart through arteries in the ventricles
- the aorta is the main artery that takes blood from the left ventricle to the body
- the main vein bringing deoxygenated blood back to the heart from the body via the right atrium is the vena cava.

Systemic circulation carries blood around the body. Every organ in the body has an arterial blood supply taking blood to it and a venous supply draining blood away when the oxygen and nutrients in it have been used up.

See also –Blood; Blood vessels; Cardiovascular system; Heart; Lungs.

ABC GUIDE TO ANATOMY AND PHYSIOLOGY

Phenylketonuria (PKU)

Phenylketonuria is an inherited metabolic condition that approximately 1 in 10000 babies are born with. Specifically, a baby with PKU has an impaired ability to metabolise or process the amino acid phenylalanine.

Phenylalanine is a necessary, natural part of the human diet. However, if a person has too much phenylalanine from protein-rich foods (meat, fish, eggs, milk) or from eating foods containing the artificial sweetener aspartame (yoghurts, ice creams, sweets) they can be poisoned. This doesn't happen to people who don't have PKU because a naturally produced enzyme, phenylalanine hydroxylase (PAH), breaks down any excess phenylalanine from food in the human body. However, people with PKU have little or no effective PAH and risk a toxic build-up of phenylalanine in their blood and brain. This can impair brain development and function and lead to intellectual disabilities, epileptic seizures and other behavioural and medical problems.

PKU is easily identified shortly after birth via a heel-prick blood test. Regular blood tests, a controlled, low-protein diet and amino acid supplements are the main treatments for PKU in childhood. A person who has this condition may stay on a low protein diet and take supplements for the rest of their life, though this isn't always necessary in adulthood. Babies and children who have regular blood tests to monitor their phenylalanine levels and who stick to a low-protein diet with amino acid supplements are likely to experience normal mental development and a normal lifespan.

See also – Foetal development.

Polycystic Ovary Syndrome

Polycystic ovary syndrome (PCOS) is a relatively common gynaecological condition that affects a woman's ovaries.

The ovaries of women with PCOS are enlarged and contain fluid-filled sacs called follicles (up to 8mm in size). Each of these under-developed sacs contain an egg that can't be released, so ovulation doesn't occur. As a result, women with PCOS have irregular periods. They also tend to produce relatively high levels of testosterone which can cause excess facial and/or body hair. Women with this condition tend to have their PCOS diagnosed in their late teens and early twenties by a GP. Weight gain, difficulties getting pregnant, excessive hair growth, thinning hair and oily skin or acne are all symptoms that young women present to their GPs before being diagnosed with this condition.

The precise cause of PCOS is not yet known. It is connected with raised hormone levels, including high levels of insulin, in the body. PCOS also seems to run in families though there is no known genetic link at present. Symptoms can be treated quite effectively through a combination of medication (to treat excessive hair growth, irregular periods and fertility problems) and lifestyle changes (losing weight, eating a balanced diet, exercising). Most women with PCOS are able to conceive with medical assistance and support.

See also – Endocrine system; Reproductive system.

Prostate cancer

The prostate is a small gland located between the penis and the bladder in the male pelvis. The prostate surrounds the urethra. It produces a thick white fluid that mixes with sperm produced by the testicles to create semen.

Prostate cancer is a slowly developing condition that causes the prostate gland to become so enlarged it affects the urethra. This causes some men to feel they need to urinate more often, makes them strain to empty their bladder and leaves them with the feeling that their bladder has not fully emptied.

Normal Prostate

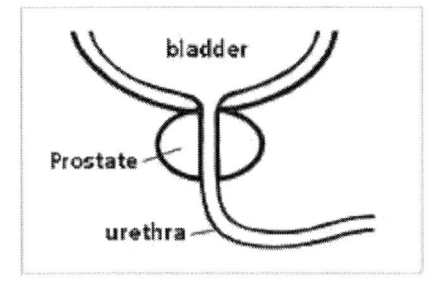

Enlarged Prostate

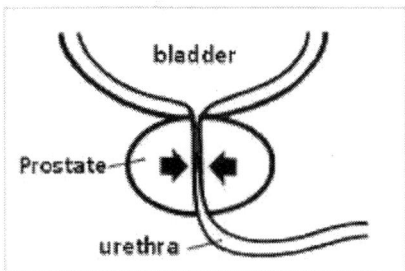

Figure 42 – An illustration of the effect an enlarged prostate has on the urethra.

HEALTH AND SOCIAL CARE

The precise cause of prostate cancer is currently unknown. The risk of doing so rises with age as it is most prevalent in men over the age of 50. Men of African-Caribbean or African descent are also more likely to develop the condition whilst men of Asian descent have a lower risk of developing it. Various blood tests, physical examination and taking a tissue biopsy are used to diagnose prostate cancer.

See also – Reproductive system.

ABC GUIDE TO ANATOMY AND PHYSIOLOGY

Renal system

The renal system consists of the kidneys, the bladder and the tubes (ureters and urethra) that carry urine out of the body. The kidneys are about 11cm long, 6cm wide and 4cm thick. They are placed higher in the body than most people imagine being tucked under the bottom of the rib cage near the spine.

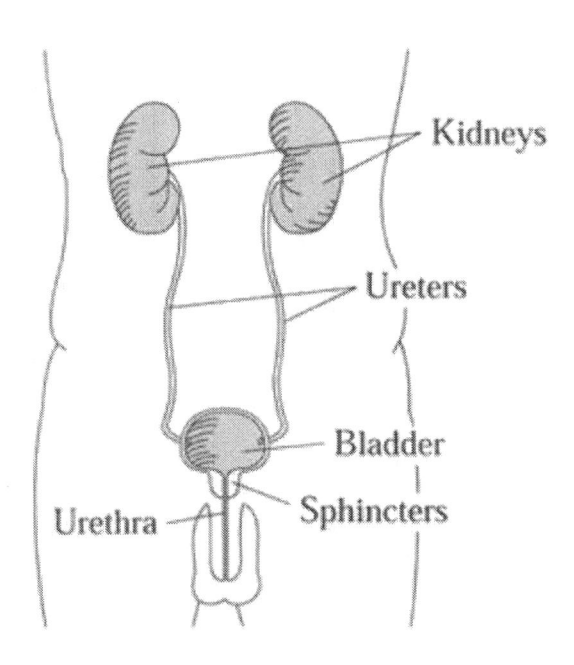

Figure 43 – The structure of the renal system.

The renal system has two functions:

- To remove waste materials made by the body from the blood and pass them out of the body in urine. This process is called excretion.

- To control the level of water in the body to make sure the concentration of solutions in the body is kept within safe limits. This process is called osmo-regulation.

We have a great deal of spare capacity in the kidneys and people have lived very healthy and active lives with only one working kidney – or even less. This is fortunate because damage to the kidneys is very serious. Since they have the job of cleaning the blood, complete kidney failure means that the blood becomes more and more toxic as waste materials build up. Eventually the body is poisoned from within if the blood isn't 'cleaned'.

How does the kidney excrete wastes?
The kidney works on the principles of ultra-filtration and selective reabsorption. This is a bit like someone looking for something in a large bag full of rubbish. The first job is to empty the bag out onto a table – this is equivalent to ultra-filtration. Then you take back all the things you want to keep – this is selective reabsorption. This strategy means the kidney can get rid of almost anything even if it does not recognise it – for example, a poison or a drug introduced into the body. It goes *out* by ultrafiltration. Only useful chemicals recognised by the kidney will be taken back *into* the body by selective reabsorption.

To carry out these tasks the kidney uses tiny tubes called nephrons. Each kidney contains over one million nephrons with a total length of over 100km. Altogether the nephrons process about 1300ml of blood every minute to make 1ml of urine and return 1299ml of clean blood back to the body.

Where does ultrafiltration occur?

Ultrafiltration takes place in the Bowman's capsule. A branch of the renal artery carries blood into a small, tangled ball of capillaries called the glomerulus tucked inside the Bowman's capsule. The blood is under pressure and most of it is squeezed through the wall of the capillaries into the space of the Bowman's capsule. The remaining blood drains away from the glomerulus along a branch of the renal vein.

Where does selective reabsorption occur?

The fluid that collects in the Bowman's capsule is called the glomerular filtrate. It passes along a tube and will eventually drain into the bladder to become urine. However, it contains many useful chemicals, and a very large amounts of water, so the body takes back these things as it passes towards the bladder. This taking back of useful chemicals is the process of selective reabsorption. Figure 40 shows the changes in the fluid as it passes along the nephron. Notice that urine contains no glucose or protein in a healthy person – these useful substances have been reabsorbed.

Figure 44 - Reabsorption by the body

	Filtered into nephrons per day	Excreted in urine per day
Blood proteins	trace	0.0g
Glucose	144g	0.0g
Salt	570g	15g
Urea	64g	30g
Water	180l	1.4l

HEALTH AND SOCIAL CARE

How does the kidney control water balance?

Adult humans produce something like 1.4 litres of urine every day and 96% of this is water. You already know that if you drink a lot of fluids you produce a lot of very dilute urine. On hot, dry days where you do not drink enough the volume of urine you produce falls but its concentration rises. How does the body control the amount and concentration of urine it produces?

Water is forced out of the blood by ultrafiltration and is reabsorbed by the kidney tubules. The amount of water reabsorbed depends on how much water the body needs to conserve. On days where you have had plenty to drink very little water is reabsorbed and you produce a lot of dilute urine. On a hot day when you have lost a lot of water through sweat, the kidneys absorb a lot of water and you produce very little concentrated urine.

See also – Kidney; Urinary tract infections (UTI); Homeostasis; Homeostatic failure.

ABC GUIDE TO ANATOMY AND PHYSIOLOGY

Reproductive system

The human reproductive system consists of the organs required to conceive and maintain a pregnancy that can result in the birth of a baby. The reproductive system is distinctive when compared to other human anatomical systems in that the reproductive organs in men are different to those in women.

The male reproductive system consists of:

- The prostate gland
- Testes
- Testicular vessels
- Penis
- Scrotum

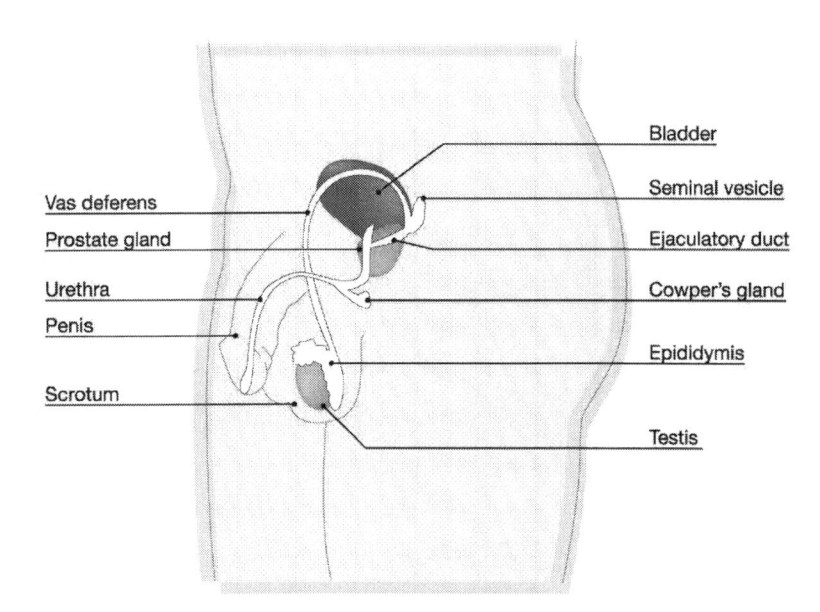

Figure 45 – An illustrated diagram of the male reproductive system.

HEALTH AND SOCIAL CARE

The male reproductive system is mainly concerned with the production of semen and its transfer into the female reproductive tract. The penis and testes, which are both located outside of the body, are key to this:

- the testes are part of both the male reproductive and endocrine systems. Their role in the reproductive system is to produce semen (and male sex hormones). They are located in the scrotum outside of the body because sperm need a cooler temperature in which to develop.
- the reproductive function of the penis is to deposit semen into the female vagina. This is achieved when, in a sexually aroused man, spongy tissue either side of the male urethra fills with blood, making the normally soft, flaccid penis stiff and erect. The penis is also an excretory organ though which urine is removed from the body.

The prostate gland, located at the base of the bladder and penis and encircling the urethra, also plays an important part in the male reproductive system. It secretes fluid that protects sperm and squeezes this into the urethra during ejaculation.

The female reproductive system consists of both internal and external parts and is more complex than the male reproductive system. The internal, functional parts of the female reproductive system are:

- the uterus is the key reproductive organ in which a foetus develops following conception. It is located in the centre of the pelvis, has thick muscular walls and a special lining called the endometrium that changes during the menstrual cycle.
- the ovaries are a small, almond-shaped pair of organs that are located each side of the pelvis. They produce the eggs (ova) every month and secrete female sex hormones (oestrogen and progesterone).

- the fallopian tubes (oviducts) are attached to the uterus and are located close to the ovaries. They are the passage down which an unfertilized egg (ovum) passes. The egg can be fertilized if recent sexual intercourse has deposited sperm in the female reproductive tract. The egg (ovum) will then move down the fallopian tube and into the uterus whether it has been fertilized or not.
- the vagina is the muscular tube that stretches and lubricates the male penis during sexual intercourse. Rhythmic movement of the vagina causes sperm to be deposited, making conception possible. The vagina together with the uterus also become the birth canal through which the baby is born during the process of childbirth.

The external structures of the female reproductive system are located in an area called the vulva. This includes the labia and clitoris. The labia are the skin flaps or folds either side of the opening to the vagina. The outer folds, the labia majora, are covered with pubic hair after puberty. The inner folds, the labia minora, do not have hair. The clitoris is a piece of tissue located above the labia that is very sensitive, fills with blood during sexual arousal and is the main source of sexual pleasure for a woman.

The main role of the female reproductive system is to produce eggs, enable their fertilization and then support and nourish the development of the foetus (and developing baby) in the uterus.

Figure 46

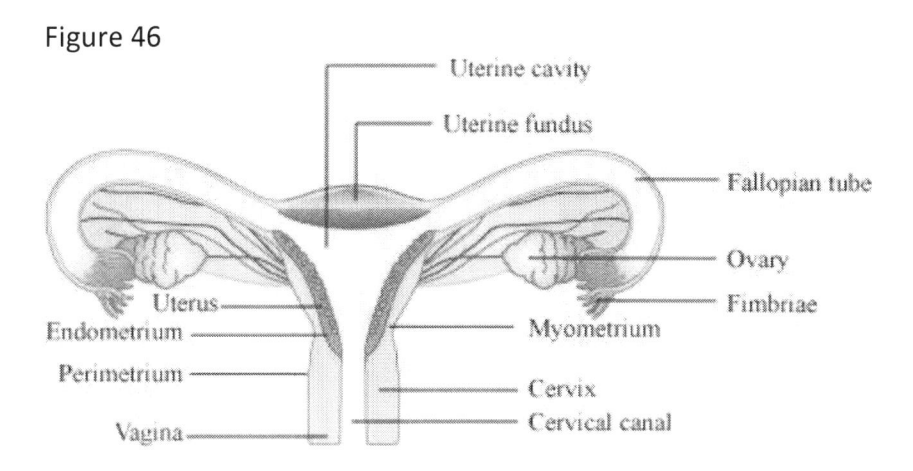

The female reproductive system

See also – Endometriosis; Polycystic ovary syndrome; Prostate cancer; Uterus;

ABC GUIDE TO ANATOMY AND PHYSIOLOGY

Respiratory system

The respiratory system includes the lungs, trachea, nose and mouth. It moves air in and out of the lungs to allow the body to absorb oxygen and remove carbon dioxide. The respiratory system works with the cardiovascular system to make sure every cell in the body has a supply of oxygen and can get rid of waste carbon dioxide. Figure 47 shows the structure of the respiratory system and the respiratory organs it consists of.

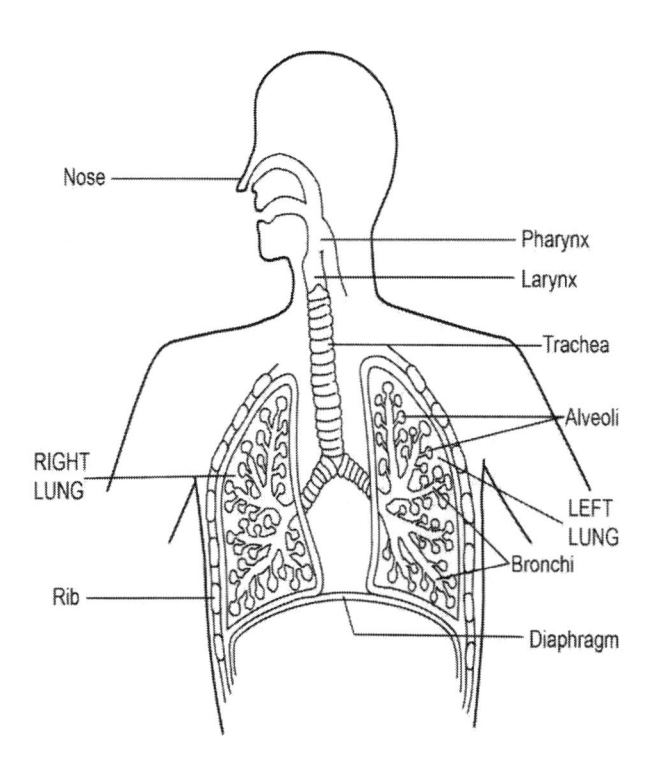

Figure 47 – The structure of the respiratory system.

See also – Asthma; Lungs; Cardiovascular system; Chronic Obstructive Pulmonary Disease; Gaseous exchange; Pneumonia

Sickle cell disease

Sickle cell disease refers to a group of inherited conditions affecting the red blood cells. People who have sickle cell disease produce red blood cells that have an unusual shape, a shorter lifespan than healthy blood cells and which can become stuck in the person's blood vessels.

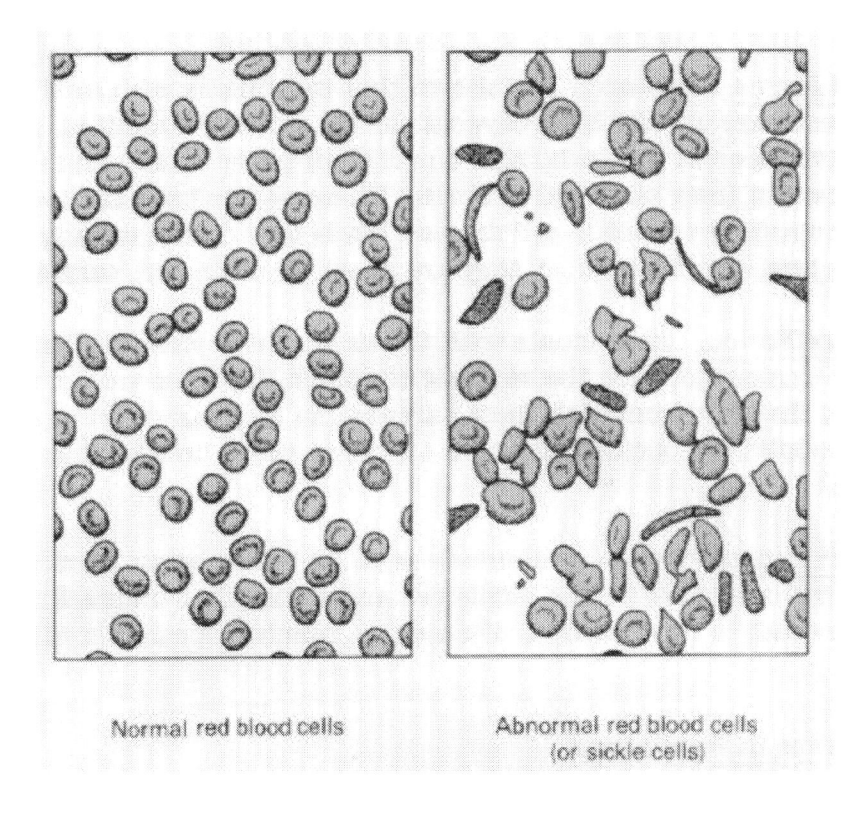

Figure 48 – An illustration of normal blood cells and sickle cells.

A faulty gene that affects how red blood cells develop causes sickle cell disease. An individual's parents may not have the disease themselves but if they are both carriers of the faulty gene, their children will have a 25% chance of being born with sickle cell disease.

Screening during pregnancy and blood tests at birth or later in life are used to identify whether the person has inherited the condition.

The main symptoms of sickle cell disease include:
- painful episodes (sickle cell crises) that can be severe and last up to a week
- increased risk and experience of serious infections
- anaemia resulting in tiredness and shortness of breath.

People who have sickle cell disease may also experience delayed growth, strokes and lung problems. Sickle cell disease is a long-term condition that requires lifelong treatment to manage the symptoms. It mainly affects people with African, Caribbean, Middle Eastern, Eastern Mediterranean and Asian heritage.

Treatment of sickle cell disease depends on the severity of the person's symptoms. Sometimes painful episodes can be managed by drinking plenty of fluids, keeping warm and taking ordinary painkillers (paracetamol, ibuprofen). However, hospital admission for blood transfusion, stronger painkillers and daily antibiotics may be needed when symptoms are more severe. Bone marrow or stem cell transplants offer potential cures for sickle cell disease but are rarely carried out because of the risks involved. Life expectancy for people with sickle cell disease tends to be shorter than average (40-60 years of age) but depends on the type and severity of sickle cell disease a person has. The milder types of the disease tend not to have an impact on life expectancy.

See also – Blood; Cells; Cell structure; Mendelian Inheritance Principles

Skeletal system

The skeletal system consists of 206 individual bones. Overall, the skeletal system consists of the bones, cartilages and joints that make up the body's hard framework. In fact, virtually any hard part of the human body is part of the human skeletal system.

The human skeleton can be divided into two main sections: the axial skeleton and the appendicular skeleton. The axial skeleton forms the axis or midline of the human body. It consists of the skull, vertebral column and thoracic (rib) cage. The appendicular skeleton consists of the bones in the limbs and the girdle muscles. This includes the shoulder girdle, the upper limbs, the pelvic girdle and the skeleton of the lower limbs (legs and feet).

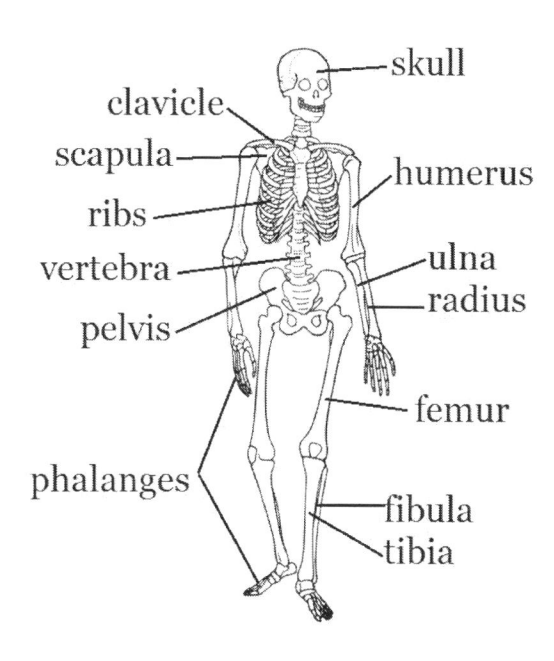

Figure 49 – Major bones in the human skeleton

ABC GUIDE TO ANATOMY AND PHYSIOLOGY

The skeleton performs a number of important functions, including providing:

- strength, support and shape to the body.
- protection for delicate organs (e.g the brain, heart and lungs etc).
- attachment and leverage for movements via joints and links to muscles and ligaments.
- red blood cells which are produced in bone marrow.
- storage of minerals (calcium and phosphate) which can enter the blood stream when the body requires them.

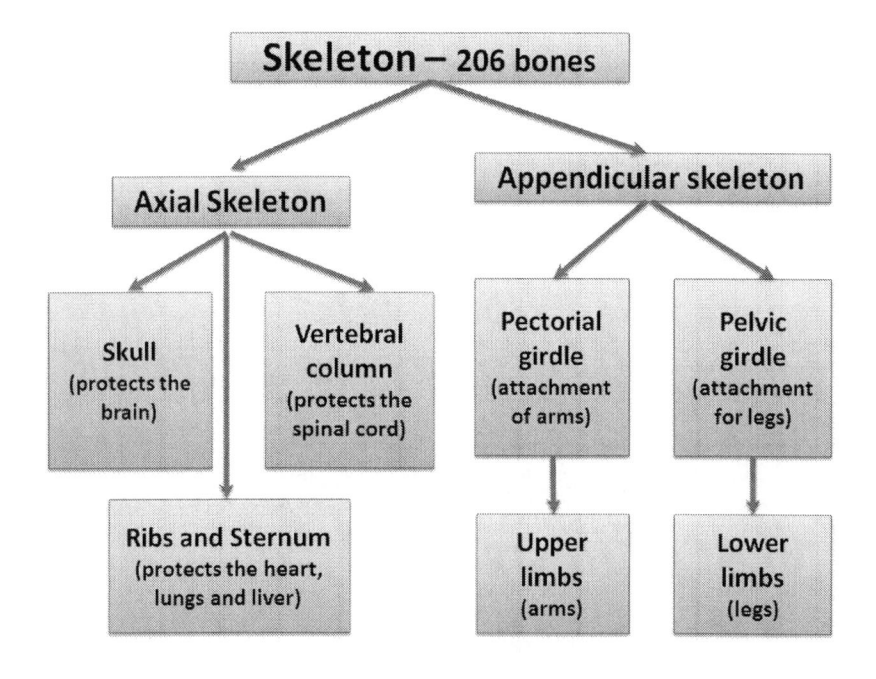

```
                    Skeleton – 206 bones
                   /                    \
          Axial Skeleton          Appendicular skeleton
          /         \              /                 \
       Skull     Vertebral     Pectorial          Pelvic
    (protects    column        girdle             girdle
    the brain)  (protects     (attachment       (attachment
                the spinal     of arms)          for legs)
                cord)
          |                        |                 |
    Ribs and Sternum            Upper             Lower
    (protects the heart,        limbs             limbs
    lungs and liver)            (arms)            (legs)
```

Figure 50 – A summary of key features of the skeletal system.

See also – Bone; Fractures; Joints; Muscle; Muscular system; Osteoarthritis; Osteoporosis.

Skin

The skin is the largest organ of the human body. It consists of two main layers: the epidermis and the dermis.

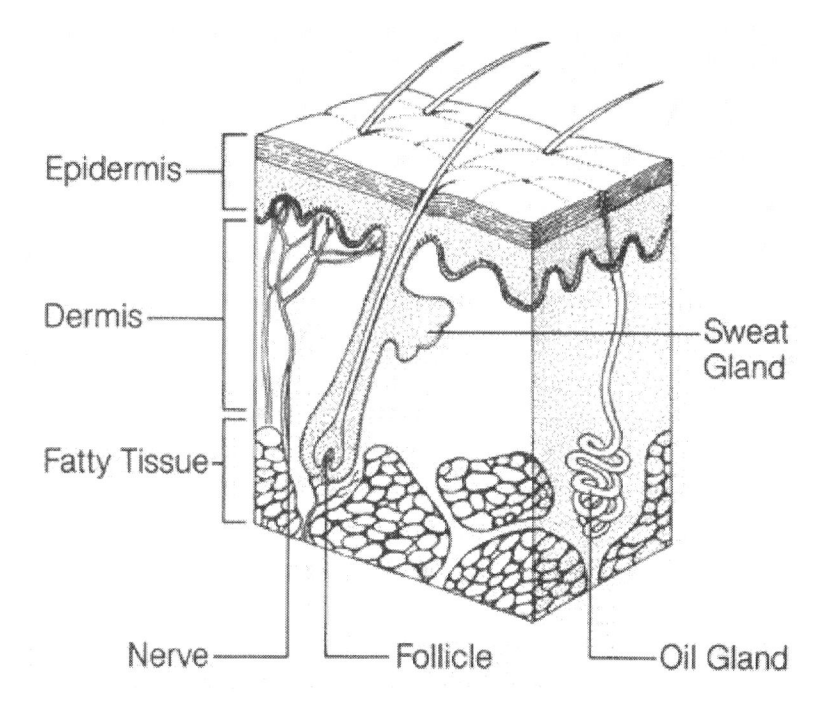

Figure 51 – A cross-sectional diagram of skin structure.

The epidermis is the outer layer of skin that you can see. It is thickest on the soles of the feet and the palms of the hand and thinnest on the eyelids and nipples. Cells are constantly being shed and replaced from the surface of the epidermis.

The dermis provides a blood supply, nutrients and fluids for the epidermis. This is the layer of skin that is connected the blood, nerves and lymph system in the body. It contains sweat and sebaceous (oil) glands, hair follicles and other living cells. The dermis is made of connective tissue and contains white collagen fibres and yellow elastic tissue known as elastin. Collagen plumps the skin up and elastin keeps it elastic and supple. Both collagen and elastin diminish as a person ages.

The skin has a number of functions including:

- Secretion
- Heat regulation
- Absorption
- Protection
- Elimination
- Sensation
- Vitamin D formation
- Melanin Formation

The function of the skin is to protect the body, maintain body temperature, receive and communicate information from the person's environment (through touch, pain and pressure, for example) and to produce sweat that carries waste products out of the body.

See also – Body temperature maintenance; Organs

Stomach

The main role of the stomach is to digest food.

The stomach is basically a j-shaped bag that stores, digests and processes food. The stomach wall consists of layers of muscle fibre with an inner mucous membrane that has lots of folds ('rugae') in it. It is quite an elastic organ, expanding and contracting in response to what it contains. When the stomach is full, the folds of the inner membrane stretch and then contract back when it empties. Mucus from the mucus membrane helps to lubricate food as it is churned in the stomach.

The food and fluids that a person ingests enter stomach via the oesophagus ('food pipe') and cardiac sphincter. The cardiac sphincter is a valve that prevents the stomach's contents from flowing back into the oesophagus. Once food enters the stomach, gastric juices (hydrochloric acid and enzymes) are released to help the digestive process. Solids are then broken down into fluids ('chyme') with the contents leaving through the pyloric sphincter and moving into the first part of the small intestine, the duodenum. Further enzymes are released in the small intestine to complete the digestion process.

See also – Alimentary canal; Digestion; Digestive system.

Stroke

The medical term for a 'stroke' is a cerebrovascular accident, summarized as a CVA by many healthcare workers. It is a serious, often life-threatening condition that occurs when the blood supply to part of a person's brain is cut off. Loss of blood supply results in the death of brain cells as they are starved of oxygen and nutrients. This can then cause serious and permanent loss of physical functioning and death.

The two main types of stroke are:
- ischaemic strokes caused by blood supply to the brain being stopped, usually due to a blood clot. Most strokes have an ischaemic cause.
- haemorrhagic strokes caused when a weakened blood vessel that supplies the brain bursts.

Transient ischaemic attack (TIA) is a similar condition to a stroke. However, the blood supply is only disrupted or stopped temporarily in a TIA. This is sometimes referred to as a 'mini-stroke' and may last between 30 minutes and several hours. A person who has a TIA may be admitted to hospital for further tests and observation as TIAs are often a warning sign that a person is at risk of having a stroke in the near future.

The main symptoms of a stroke can be identified using the FAST test. That is, the person's:

- Face may have dropped on one side
- Arms will be weak or numb, on one or both sides
- Speech may be slurred or garbled
- Time is critical, so phone 999 if the person has any of these symptoms.

In addition, a person who has a stroke may also experience:

- a sudden, severe headache
- paralysis on one side of their body
- difficulty swallowing
- blurred vision or loss of vision
- dizziness, poor balance and lack of coordination
- confusion and difficulty understanding others
- loss of consciousness

High blood pressure, smoking, being overweight, lack of exercise, high cholesterol levels and poor diet are all risk factors for stroke. Older people and people from south Asian, African and Caribbean backgrounds also have a higher risk of experiencing a stroke, probably because of their predisposition to high blood pressure.

See also – Brain; Blood pressure; Blood vessels; Cardiovascular system.

Tissues

A tissue is a group of cells all of the same type. For example, the cells lining the inner surface of the gut form a tissue, muscle cells in a muscle form a tissue. The cells in a tissue all have the same structure and function.

There are four main types of human tissue:

A. epithelial tissue are thin sheets that line and cover a variety of body structures, such as the intestines, for example.

B. connective tissue is tough, fibrous and holds parts of the body together. Ligaments and tendons are largely connective tissue.

C. muscular tissue is present in all muscles, including the heart, and has the ability to contract and produce movement.

D. nervous tissue consists of neurons that conduct impulses enabling communication between the brain and different parts of the body.

HEALTH AND SOCIAL CARE

(A) Epithelial tissue

(B) Connective tissue

(C) Muscle tissue

(D) Nervous tissue

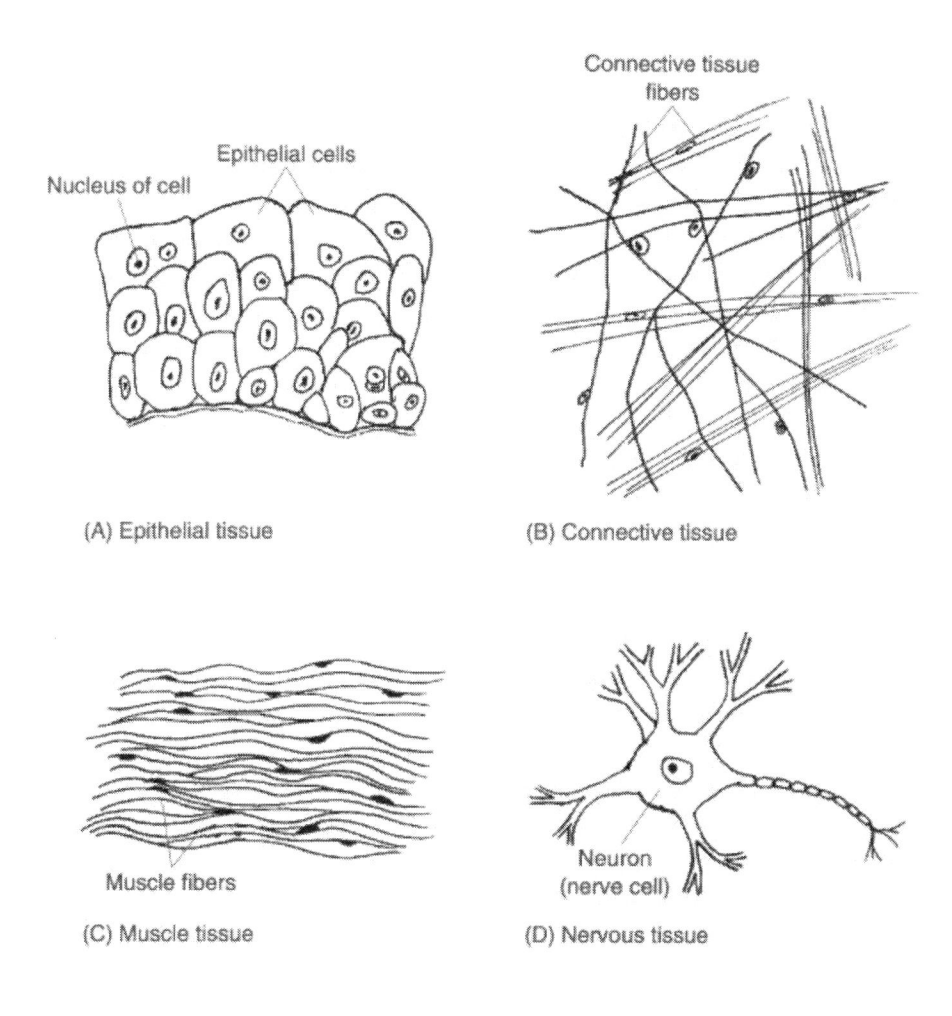

Figure 52 – An illustration of different types of cells

See also – Cells, Cell structure; Connective tissue; Epithelial tissue; Nervous tissue; Muscle; Organs.

ABC GUIDE TO ANATOMY AND PHYSIOLOGY

Uterus

The uterus is the major female organ that enables sexual reproduction to occur. It is positioned in the pelvic area of the body, between the bladder and the rectum. In popular, non-medical language it is generally referred to as the womb.

Anatomically, the uterus consists of the:

- endometrium, the inner lining of the uterus
- myometrium, the middle, muscular layer
- perimetrium, the outer layer.

At one end, the uterus is connected to the cervix and via this the vagina. At the other end, it is connected to the fallopian tubes. The function or purpose of the uterus is to nourish and support the growth or a foetus during pregnancy.

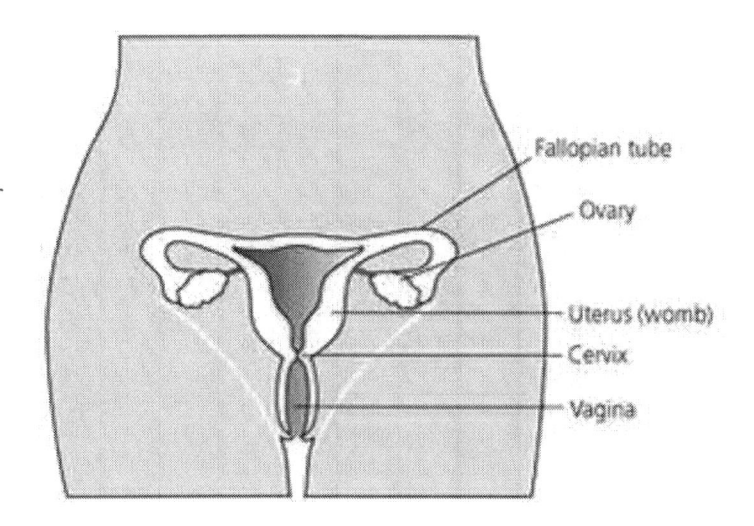

Figure 53 – The anatomy of the uterus

HEALTH AND SOCIAL CARE

When a woman menstruates, her ovaries release eggs into the fallopian tubes. These eggs travel via the fallopian tubes to the uterus. If fertised by male sperm, the eggs will bind to the wall of the uterus and the foetus will begin developing. The uterus must nourish and protect the developing foetus until birth occurs. The myometrium layer of the uterus assists with the birth process, pushing the baby out of the uterus into the cervix and vagina.

See also – Endometriosis; Foetal development; Reproductive system

ABC GUIDE TO ANATOMY AND PHYSIOLOGY

UTI (Urinary Tract Infection)

The urinary tract is the part of the body where urine is made and processed. It consists of the kidneys, the ureters, the bladder and the urethra. The kidneys make urine out of waste products drawn from the blood. This then passes down the ureter tubes to the bladder where it is stored. Urine is then expelled from the body through the urethra tube that connects to the bladder.

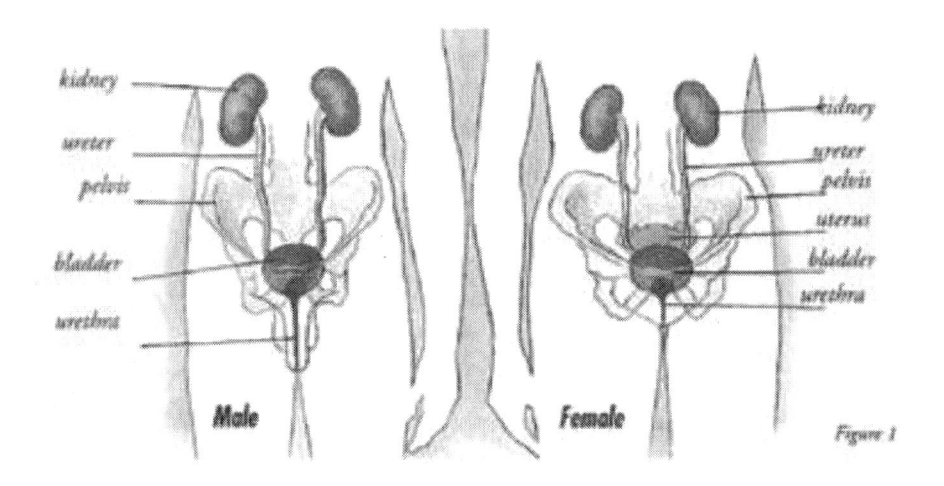

Figure 54 - The male and female urinary systems

A UTI (Urinary Tract Infection) occurs when part of the urinary tract becomes infected by bacteria. Infection of the bladder (cystitis) or urethra (urethritis) are known as lower urinary tract infections. These are more common and less serious than upper urinary tract infections. In fact, UTI infections are very common, usually short-term, minor health problems that resolve quickly. The main symptoms of a UTI are:

- a painful, sometimes burning, feeling when urinating

- needing to urinate a lot (frequency)
- pain in the lower abdomen (tummy) area
- strong or offensive smelling urine

Generally, these symptoms go away after a few days without any treatment. However, a GP (family doctor) may also prescribe a course of antibiotics to clear up the infection. Women are more likely to get UTIs than men. Those who repeatedly experience UTIs may be prescribed long-term antibiotics as a preventative measure. Complications of UTI are rare but people with lowered immunity or who have diabetes or kidney problems are at higher risk of blood poisoning and kidney failure.

See also – Bladder; Kidneys; Renal system.

Printed in Great Britain
by Amazon